FACTS AT YOUR
FINGERTIPS

VIETNAM WAR

FACTS AT YOUR FINGERTIPS

VIETNAM WAR

BROWN
BEAR
BOOKS

Published by Brown Bear Books

An imprint of
The Brown Reference Group Ltd
68 Topstone Road
Redding
Connecticut
06896
USA

www.brownreference.com

Library of Congress Cataloging-in-Publication Data
available upon request.

ISBN-13 978-1-933834-51-1

Author: Leo Daugherty
Editorial Director: Lindsey Lowe
Senior Managing Editor: Tim Cooke
Designer: Sarah Williams
Editor: Peter Darman

Printed in the United States of America

CONTENTS

INTRODUCTION

In the 19th and early 20th centuries the French ruled all of Vietnam. The Vietnamese resented being ruled by foreigners, and there were uprisings against the French between 1930 and 1931. They were organized by the Vietnam National Party, but were easily crushed. However, the more militant Indochinese Communist Party became stronger. By the outbreak of World War II in 1939 it was the dominant nationalist party in Vietnam. The fall of France to the Germans in 1940 weakened French power in Vietnam, and in the same year Japanese troops moved into the country and effectively ruled it. But when Japan was defeated by the Allies, Ho Chi Minh declared himself president of Vietnam on August 16, 1945. Following elections in the north in January 1946, Ho became the president of the Democratic Republic of Vietnam (DRV). On March 6, 1946, he signed an agreement with France that recognized the DRV as a free state (French troops had reoccupied the south of Vietnam). However, France refused to deal with him. The French then set up a provisional government in the South called the Republic of Cochin-China. This led to the outbreak of war between the North and France in December 1946.

North and South Vietnam

After eight years of war, France was defeated. The signing of the Geneva Peace Accords (May 1954), between the French and the communists meant Vietnam was divided into two halves. The United States replaced the French as the supporter of the Republic of Vietnam (RVN)—South Vietnam. The Soviet Union and the People's Republic of China performed a similar role with the communist northern half, known as the Democratic Republic of Vietnam (DRVN)—North Vietnam—led by Ho Chi Minh.

To help South Vietnam, the Americans set up the Military Assistance Group, Vietnam. U.S. military advisors from the army, navy, air force, and Marine Corps went to Vietnam to instruct and train the Army of the Republic of Vietnam (ARVN).

As the new South Vietnam struggled to maintain its independence, in late 1957 North Vietnamese leaders agreed on a strategy designed to unify the

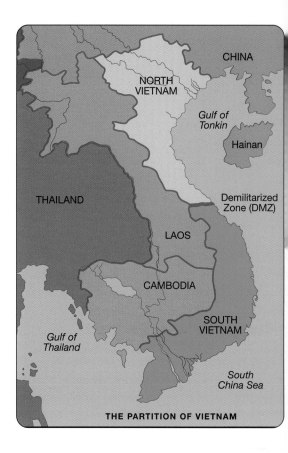

THE PARTITION OF VIETNAM

country under the banner of communism. Meanwhile, with growing U.S. backing, South Vietnamese President Ngo Dinh Diem tightened his already dictatorial rule. This alienated both his generals and the civilian population of the South. U.S. military advisors tried to restrain Diem, but politicians in Washington, D.C., began to worry about a communist take-over. They therefore poured equipment and troops into the South to help the ARVN.

On November 2, 1963, both Diem and his brother Nhu were brutally murdered in a military revolt led by South Vietnamese General Duong Van Minh. Diem's assassination began a series of events that would eventually lead to the full-scale commitment of U.S. combat troops. Even as the United States tried to stabilize the situation in South Vietnam's capital, Saigon, President John F. Kennedy, Jr., was likewise assassinated while visiting Dallas, Texas, on November 22, 1963. His successor, President Lyndon B. Johnson, inherited from the Kennedy Administration a growing U.S. commitment to safeguard South Vietnam. By the end of 1963, there were around 16,500 U.S. troops and advisors serving in South Vietnam. More than 489 of them were killed in action while "advising" the ARVN.

War between North and South

As the political situation in South Vietnam worsened, the Johnson Administration struggled to find a military solution to what was now turning into a full-scale war by the combined forces of the National Liberation Front (NLF), or Viet Cong (VC), and North Vietnamese Army (NVA). The VC were guerrillas who operated inside South Vietnam itself. When North Vietnamese vessels allegedly fired on two U.S. warships in the Gulf of Tonkin off the North Vietnamese coastline in August 1964, the Johnson Administration ordered the first bombings of North Vietnam in what would be termed Operation Rolling Thunder. This was the codeword for the massive U.S. air offensive designed to punish the North for its attacks on the South and halt its support for the Viet Cong.

Despite massive bombings by aircraft launched from U.S. Navy aircraft carriers offshore in the Gulf of Tonkin and from airfields in Thailand and Guam, the war in South Vietnam continued to get worse. When Viet Cong and North Vietnamese troops attacked two U.S. air bases at Bien Hoa (November 1, 1964) and Quinhon (February 10, 1965), President Johnson stepped up the growing bombing campaign against North Vietnamese forces. He also agreed to a request by General William C. Westmoreland, Commanding General, U.S. Military Assistance Command, Vietnam (MACV), to send U.S. Marines to guard the vital airfield at Da Nang, along South Vietnam's coast. The sending of U.S. ground and air forces signaled the start of American involvement in a war that would last nearly a decade (1965–1975).

A napalm bomb dropped by a U.S. aircraft explodes during an attack against Viet Cong guerrillas in South Vietnam. Napalm is a gel that burns easily and sticks fast to anything it touches.

Despite the arrival of a massive amount of U.S. military assistance and personnel, the political situation inside South Vietnam continued to deteriorate. South Vietnam's president Ngo Dinh Diem faced both a Viet Cong (VC) guerrilla war and growing dissatisfaction with his rule by the Buddhists who made up the bulk of the population in the South. After a failed crackdown on Buddhist monks, some of whom set fire to themselves to dramatize their opposition to Diem, the South Vietnamese Army (with American approval) launched a coup d'état (revolt) against the president and his brother, both of whom were killed in the first week of November 1963. However, coup after coup failed to bring stability to the political situation in Saigon, the South's capital. Despite the political instability, the growing strength of the North, and a change of leadership in Washington, D.C., after the death of President John F. Kennedy, the U.S. response to the continued aggression from the Viet Cong and North Vietnam was to increase its military support to South Vietnam, especially to the Army of the Republic of Vietnam (ARVN). By the end of 1964, the United States Military Assistance Command, Vietnam (MACV), under General William C. Westmoreland, had grown to more than 20,000 men.

Increasing American aid

In 1964 the U.S. Marine contingent numbered over 800 men in Vietnam. The bulk of these were located in South Vietnam's I Corps Tactical Zone (ICTZ), which consisted of the five northern provinces nearest to the so-called Demilitarized Zone (DMZ), next to North Vietnam. Some 60 Marine advisors had been attached to the ARVN's 1st and 2d Divisions. Meanwhile the so-called Shu Fly unit, reinforced with a U.S. Marine rifle company, provided airfield perimeter security at the Da Nang Air Base, south of the city of Da Nang along South Vietnam's extended coastline. Twenty U.S. Marines served with the Vietnamese Marine Corps and

This is an A-4 Skyhawk, which was used in the Vietnam War by the U.S. Navy and Marines. It was a single-seat aircraft designed for ground-attack missions. The long probe allowed the aircraft to be refueled in midair.

a detachment of Marines served in the Marine Embassy Guard and on the MACV staff in Saigon.

With President Lyndon B. Johnson now committed to the defense of South Vietnam, there was increasing talk in Washington, D.C., of sending combat troops to South Vietnam to defend U.S. installations there. After the Gulf of Tonkin incidents in August 1964, the United States became drawn into ground fighting and Johnson ordered the first air strikes against targets in North Vietnam in Operation Rolling Thunder. After South Vietnamese Army units suffered a series of defeats on the ground, Westmoreland and the U.S. Joint Chiefs of Staff approved the sending of U.S. Marines to South Vietnam. The U.S. commitment to South Vietnam was now complete.

A full-scale war

By the time 1965 came to an end, the war in Vietnam had clearly become America's War. More than 148,300 combat and support troops had been deployed to South Vietnam. From the Central Highlands to the coastal plains, United States soldiers and Marines battled the VC and the North Vietnamese Army (NVA), while airmen and sailors carried out a long-term bombing campaign of North Vietnam. They also bombed the communist supply line which ran through Laos and Cambodia, which became infamous as the Ho Chi Minh Trail.

On the ground the ARVN had many soldiers—500,000 in 1965 rising to one million in the 1970s—but many of its officers were corrupt and poorly motivated. In contrast, the troops of the NVA, numbering around 400,000, were well trained, led, and had high morale. Inside South Vietnam itself the VC was at least 10,000 strong in 1965. Nicknamed "Charlie" by the Americans, most VC guerrillas were recruited in the South, but received weapons, guidance, and reinforcements from North Vietnamese Army soldiers who had infiltrated into South Vietnam. For the most part, the VC fought a guerrilla war of ambush, terrorism, and sabotage, using small units to hold the countryside, leaving the main population centers to government authorities. The VC was indeed an elusive enemy.

At the end of 1962, the South Vietnamese government decided to attempt to regain control of a large part of the Mekong Delta, large areas of which were controlled by the Viet Cong (VC). The attack was to take place in Western Dinh Tuong Province, near the village of Ap Bac. The plan was to pin down VC forces and destroy them.

The Viet Cong was ready and waiting

However, elements of both the VC 514th Regional Battalion and the 261st Main Force Battalion were at Ap Bac—a total of more than 300 fighters. Also, the VC intercepted ARVN radio transmissions that tipped them off about the intended attack against AP Bac.

At 07:30 hours on January 2, 1963, the first troops of the 7th Division arrived by H-21 helicopters (shown below) in the rice paddies to the north of Ap Bac. The pilots of the 10 H-21s landed too close to the trees, and their aircraft immediately came under small-arms fire. Three H-21s and one of the five escorting UH-1 gunships were shot down. The Vietnamese troops piled out of the aircraft and took cover, remaining there for the remainder of the day.

In the south, two ARVN battalions ran into VC troops, came under fire, and halted. They began firing at the Viet Cong, with little result but a slow and steady stream of killed and wounded.

All the South Vietnamese troops were now pinned down, and even an attack by M113 armored personnel carriers failed. Using good fire discipline, the VC kept the attackers pinned down until darkness fell, when they gradually slipped away.

A female Viet Cong guerrilla in the Mekong Delta. Her and hundreds like her defeated the ARVN at Ap Bac in January 1963.

BATTLE OF AP BAC

Location   Ap Bac, Mekong Delta, South Vietnam

Date   January 2, 1963

Casualties   Viet Cong:18 killed, 39 wounded; South Vietnamese: 80 killed, 100 wounded

Commanders and forces   Viet Cong: 514th Regional Battalion and the 261st Main Force Battalion (Hai Hoang); South Vietnamese: 7th Division (Colonel Bui Dinh Dam)

Key actions   The failure of the ARVN troops who were landed by helicopter to attack the VC lost the South the battle.

Key effects   The Viet Cong had stood up to massive firepower from helicopter-delivered machine guns and rockets, artillery, tactical air power, and heavy machine guns of the armored personnel carriers. They had coolly fought the battle on their own terms; and had broken contact on their initiative. It was a communist victory.

VIET CONG TERRORISM

The *Viet Nam Cong San* (Vietnamese Communists) was a guerrilla force that, with the support of the North Vietnamese Army, fought against both South Vietnam (late 1950s to 1975) and the United States (early 1960s to 1973). Emerging in the mid-1950s as a collection of various groups opposed to the government of President Diem, the Viet Cong became in 1960 the military arm of the National Liberation Front (NLF). In 1969 the NLF brought together groups in the areas of South Vietnam that were controlled by the Viet Cong (VC) to form the Provisional Revolutionary Government (PRG). The movement's principal objectives were the overthrow of the South Vietnamese Government and the reunification of Vietnam. To achieve this aim the VC used terrorism.

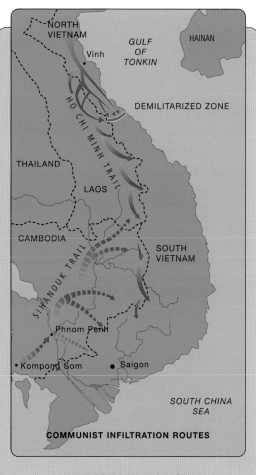

VIET CONG TERRORISM

Location	South Vietnam
Date	1964
Commanders and forces	The entire Viet Cong
Casualties	Unknown

Key actions In February 1964 the VC launched an offensive in Tay Ninh province and the Mekong Delta; in the ensuing fighting, hundreds of government troops were reported dead or missing.

Key effects The NVA and VC appeared to be building up their strength for a final offensive against the largely demoralized armed forces and unstable government in South Vietnam. The VC and NVA were accomplishing all of this despite the massive infusion of U.S. military and economic assistance. Indeed, the presence of U.S. advisors was having a negligible effect on the ARVN's ability to deal with the insurgency.

Viet Cong tactics

The terror tactics used by the VC were many and varied. In the countryside, the guerrillas would attack isolated villages at night and murder village leaders. They also killed peasants who opposed them, peasants who cooperated with the government, policemen, tax collectors, teachers, and government employees. Spreading fear was a key communist tactic. Victims would be hauled out in front of the entire village and made to beg for their lives, before being shot, strangled or stabbed by their tormentors. The bodies would then be left where they fell. The VC would then disappear into the countryside, but the villagers knew that they might return the next night or the night after that. In this way villagers were forced to support the VC, even if they were reluctant to do so.

In the cities the VC planted bombs designed to spread fear and undermined the authority of the government. Saigon, the capital, was a high priority for VC attacks. On February 16, 1964, for example, three Americans were killed and 32 injured when a VC bomb exploded in the Kinh Do movie theater. Five days later the Saigon–Da Nang train was derailed by a bomb, resulting in 11 people killed and 18 seriously injured.

The VC waged an effective terror campaign in the South in 1964. Between February and August 1964, for example, the VC killed 429 local South Vietnamese officials and kidnapped 482 others. This resulted in large parts of South Vietnam coming under the control of the VC. Indeed, by August 1964 the Viet Cong, strongly supported by regular army units from North Vietnam, held the military initiative in South Vietnam. The VC and NVA controlled much of the countryside.

NAM DONG

U.S. tactics to oppose the Viet Cong (VC) involved establishing small teams of U.S. Special Forces soldiers (Green Berets) in fortified villagers. The Green Berets would train and arm the villagers to defend their homes, making it impossible for the VC to terrorize them. However, the communists continued to launch attacks to wipe the villages out. One such village was at Nam Dong, south of Khe Sanh and only 15 miles (24 km) from Laos. On the night of July 5, 1964, Captain

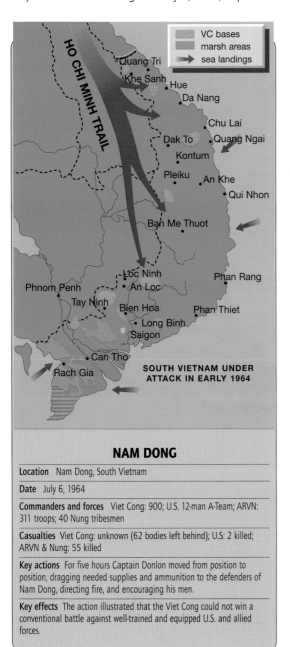

SOUTH VIETNAM UNDER ATTACK IN EARLY 1964

VC bases
marsh areas
sea landings

NAM DONG

Location	Nam Dong, South Vietnam
Date	July 6, 1964
Commanders and forces	Viet Cong: 900; U.S. 12-man A-Team; ARVN: 311 troops; 40 Nung tribesmen
Casualties	Viet Cong: unknown (62 bodies left behind); U.S: 2 killed; ARVN & Nung: 55 killed
Key actions	For five hours Captain Donlon moved from position to position, dragging needed supplies and ammunition to the defenders of Nam Dong, directing fire, and encouraging his men.
Key effects	The action illustrated that the Viet Cong could not win a conventional battle against well-trained and equipped U.S. and allied forces.

Roger Donlon's 12-man Special Forces Team A-726 stood ready at Nam Dong for a VC attack. In previous days there had been indications that something was about to happen. Patrols outside the camp had noticed increased activity and the villagers seemed nervous and scared. The previous morning a U.S. patrol reported finding the corpses of two village chiefs who had been friendly to the Americans.

The communists attack

At 02:26 hours Donlon finished his rounds. The Green Berets were ready, and so too were the 311 South Vietnamese soldiers and 40 Nungs (ethnic Chinese who worked with the Special Forces) that made up his garrison. Suddenly, mortar, small-arms, and machine-gun fire erupted all around. Nam Dong was under attack.

Donlon raced for one of the mortar pits, but an enemy mortar shell exploded near his feet, tossing him into the air. Donlon, dizzy but uninjured, crawled into the mortar pit. Then a third mortar round exploded near him. Donlon lost his other boot and all of his equipment except his rifle and two magazines. Worse, shrapnel had seriously wounded him in his left arm and stomach. He managed to force his battered body to another mortar pit from which he could see enemy soldiers only 60 ft (18.2 m) from the main gate.

Upon entering one of his team's own mortar pits and finding most of the men wounded, he directed their withdrawal to a position 90 ft (27.4 m) away. As they retreated he provided cover fire for them. Then, while attempting to drag the severely wounded "Pop" Alamo from the same position, Donlon was hit again by mortar fire that wounded him in the shoulder and killed his team sergeant.

When morning dawned the five-hour battle had left 55 of the South Vietnamese and Nung defenders dead and another 65 wounded. "Pop" Alamo and John Houston were also dead, never to witness the birth of children their pregnant wives were bearing at home. But the defenders at Nam Dong had held through the night, outnumbered at least 3 to 1 by a reinforced battalion of enemy soldiers. Donlon's team would become one of the most highly decorated units in U.S. Army history.

GULF OF TONKIN INCIDENT

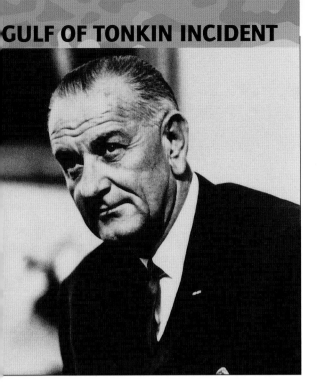

U.S. President Lyndon Johnson ordered attacks against North Vietnam in retaliation for the incident in the Gulf of Tonkin.

Late in the afternoon of August 2, about 28 miles (45 km) off the North Vietnamese coastline in the Gulf of Tonkin, the USS *Maddox* was attacked by three North Vietnamese boats. One boat was disabled, the second retreated to the north, and the third boat, hit by at least one shot, passed across the bow of the *Maddox* and sprayed it with 12.7-mm machine-gun fire. On August 4, the *Maddox*, joined by the USS *C. Turner Joy*, was attacked by North Vietnamese naval boats. In self-defense, the U.S. ships opened fire with their 5-in naval guns. In the confusion that subsequently occurred, the *C. Turner Joy* and *Maddox* sank one, possibly two, North Vietnamese boats.

GULF OF TONKIN INCIDENT

Location Gulf of Tonkin

Date August 2–4, 1964

Commanders and forces USS *Maddox* and USS *C. Turner Joy*

Casualties North Vietnamese: unknown; U.S.: none

Key actions The U.S. ships successfully evaded enemy fire

Key effects The United States Congress approved the Southeast Asia Resolution (Senate vote 88–2, and House of Representatives 414–0). This so-called "Gulf of Tonkin Resolution" gave President Johnson permission to take all the steps that he deemed necessary in order to protect U.S. personnel and U.S. interests within Vietnam.

ATTACK ON VINH

A U.S. Navy attack aircraft is refueled prior to an attack against North Vietnamese targets in August 1964.

President Johnson announced to the public that the United States was making a measured response to the North Vietnamese attacks in the Gulf of Tonkin, but did not intend to provoke a war. Sixty-four aircraft were launched from the decks of the U.S. Navy's aircraft carriers USS *Ticonderoga* and *Constellation* in Operation Pierce Arrow. They inflicted severe damage on the North Vietnamese gunboat and torpedo fleet, destroying eight vessels and damaging 21 others. Smoke from the Vinh petroleum storage areas rose 14,000 ft (4267 m) into the air. U.S. Navy planes estimated that they had destroyed over 90 percent of the fuel stored there. The U.S. Navy lost two jets from the USS *Constellation* to enemy antiaircraft fire, while two other jets were hit but were not shot down.

ATTACK ON VINH

Location Vinh, North Vietnam

Date August 5, 1964

Commanders and forces North Vietnam: unknown; U.S.: Attack Squadrons 144 and 145

Casualties North Vietnamese: unknown; U.S.: 1 killed

Key actions The attack achieved complete suprise.

Key effects The operation marked a further escalation in U.S. involvement in Vietnam.

OPERATION ROLLING THUNDER

Operation Rolling Thunder began on February 24, 1965, when over 100 American aircraft attacked targets in North Vietnam. Scheduled to last eight weeks, Rolling Thunder instead went on for three years.

The first U.S. air strikes also hit the Ho Chi Minh Trail. Throughout the war, the trail was heavily bombed by American jets with little actual success in halting the tremendous flow of soldiers and supplies from the North. After each attack, bomb damage along the trail was repaired by female construction crews.

The majority of bombs dropped in South Vietnam targeted Viet Cong and North Vietnamese Army positions. In North Vietnam, military targets included fuel depots and factories. The North Vietnamese reacted to the air strikes by spreading their factories and supply bases among many locations.

OPERATION ROLLING THUNDER

Location North and South Vietnam

Date February 24, 1965, to October 31, 1968

Commanders and forces North Vietnamese Air Force: 700 aircraft (Nguyen Van Tien); U.S. Air Force: 1,000 aircraft (General LeMay)

Casualties North Vietnamese: unknown; U.S.: 835 killed, captured, or missing

Key actions The Johnson administration imposed strict limits on the targets that could be attacked, fearing that China and the Soviet Union might intervene if the North Vietnamese faced defeat. Consequently, the administration tried to punish the North without provoking the two nations believed to be its protectors.

Key effects When Rolling Thunder failed to weaken the enemy's will after the first several weeks, the purpose of the campaign began to change. By the end of 1965, the Johnson administration still used air power as an attempt to change North Vietnamese policy, but bombing was directed against the flow of men and supplies from the North, thus damaging the enemy militarily while warning him of the danger of greater destruction if he maintained the present aggressive course.

BATTLE FOR BINH DINH PROVINCE

Some of the fiercest fighting in 1964 took place in Binh Dinh Province, located in the middle of communist Military District 5. General Westmoreland, commander of the U.S. war effort in Vietnam, had urged South Vietnamese Army commanders to break down their forces into small units and spread them out to provide as many villages with protection as possible. But communist units attacked these small units one by one. Lacking any large reserve, government forces were either wiped out or forced to retreat.

Search and destroy

As well as protecting villagers, Westmoreland also wanted the ARVN to carry out a so-called "search and destroy" policy. Search and destroy operations began in 1964, before U.S. ground forces were committed to the conflict. These operations were conducted to locate the North Vietnamese Army (NVA) and Viet Cong (VC) units in and around their base areas and to attack them with heavy firepower (artillery and air attacks) and maneuver by infantry units. The communist ability to attack the South's populated areas depended heavily on being able to set up bases nearby. Therefore, if these bases could be destroyed then the VC would find it very difficult to launch operations in the South.

However, the ARVN often discovered that in 1964 the VC was so strong that its units often stood their ground and defeated ARVN forces.

BATTLE FOR BINH DINH PROVINCE

Location Binh Dinh Province

Date October to November 1964

Commanders and forces North Vietnamese Army, NVA 2d Regiment and 409th Sapper Battalion, plus unknown number of Viet Cong guerrillas

Casualties Unknown

Key actions The Viet Cong and NVA were able to mount a sustained and highly effective offensive throughout a heavily populated central coastal province.

Key effects In a series of attacks and ambushes, ARVN forces were either overrun, destroyed, or driven back into their fortified camps. Control of the countryside was lost and the initiative passed to the Viet Cong. By the end of October, most of the second largest province in South Vietnam was under VC control, and the government presence was limited to some towns and the capital, Qui Nhon.

The Battle of Binh Gia was part of a larger communist campaign conducted by the Viet Cong (VC) from December 28, 1964, to January 1, 1965, in Phuoc Tuy Province (Binh Gia was a village located southeast of Saigon). Elements of the VC 9th Division, led by the 514th Battalion, began their assault during the early morning of December 28. They overran several ARVN outposts and quickly overwhelmed the local militia forces. Later that morning, two South Vietnamese Ranger units counterattacked but were unable to clear the enemy from their positions. They advanced to within 984 ft (300 m) of Binh Gia village until a VC battalion forced them to withdraw.

Heavy ARVN casualties

Reinforcements from the 30th and 33rd South Vietnamese Rangers arrived on December 29, but they were unable to dislodge the well-entrenched VC. After some heavy fighting the Ranger battalions were decimated by VC machine-gun fire. On the morning of December 30, the South Vietnamese 4th Marine Battalion landed by helicopter and attacked. They recaptured Binh Gia, but the VC was nowhere to be seen. Later that day, a U.S. Army gunship was shot down, killing four crewmen.

One company (around 100 soldiers) from the 4th Marine Battalion was sent to the crash site to try to recover the bodies, but the South Vietnamese were ambushed again. On the morning of December 31, the entire 4th Marine Battalion moved westward in an attempt to rescue the trapped company. At the site of the crash, the 4th Marine Battalion and their American advisors discovered fresh graves. They also found themselves in a deadly ambush. VC soldiers launched vicious attacks on the ARVN, and further reinforcements from the 29th, 30th, and 33rd ARVN Ranger Battalions rushed to the scene. They too were ambushed and suffered huge casualties. The latest battle resulted in the deaths of 35 ARVN officers, 112 Marines and 71 wounded bringing the total casualties to more than 300. On January 1 further ARVN reinforcements arrived, but they were too late to make a difference.

A change in Viet Cong tactics

Unlike their usual tactics, the Viet Cong forces at Binh Gia did not slip away from the battlefield during the hours of darkness. Instead they held the field for four days and resisted all ARVN attacks. Binh Gia should have been an eye opener for the ARVN forces and their U.S. advisors.

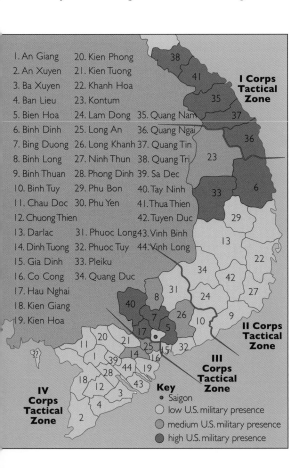

1. An Giang	20. Kien Phong
2. An Xuyen	21. Kien Tuong
3. Ba Xuyen	22. Khanh Hoa
4. Ban Lieu	23. Kontum
5. Bien Hoa	24. Lam Dong
6. Binh Dinh	25. Long An
7. Bing Duong	26. Long Khanh
8. Binh Long	27. Ninh Thun
9. Binh Thuan	28. Phong Dinh
10. Binh Tuy	29. Phu Bon
11. Chau Doc	30. Phu Yen
12. Chuong Thien	
13. Darlac	31. Phuoc Long
14. Dinh Tuong	32. Phuoc Tuy
15. Gia Dinh	33. Pleiku
16. Co Cong	34. Quang Duc
17. Hau Nghia	
18. Kien Giang	
19. Kien Hoa	
35. Quang Nam	36. Quang Ngai
37. Quang Tin	38. Quang Tri
39. Sa Dec	40. Tay Ninh
41. Thua Thien	42. Tuyen Duc
43. Vinh Binh	44. Vinh Long

Key
● Saigon
○ low U.S. military presence
◐ medium U.S. military presence
● high U.S. military presence

I Corps Tactical Zone
II Corps Tactical Zone
III Corps Tactical Zone
IV Corps Tactical Zone

BATTLE OF BINH GIA

Location   Phuoc Tuy Province

Date   December 28, 1964–January 1, 1965

Commanders and forces   Viet Cong: 271st and 272d Regiments; ARVN: 1st Airborne Battalion, 3rd Airborne Battalion, 7th Airborne Battalion, 30th Ranger Battalion, 33rd Ranger Battalion, 35th Ranger Battalion, 38th Ranger Battalion, two artillery platoons, and one section of M-24 tanks in support

Casualties   VC: 32 killed; ARVN: 201 killed

Key actions   The ARVN 33rd Ranger Battalion was destroyed.

Key effects   The Viet Cong demonstrated that, when well supplied with military supplies from North Vietnam, it had the ability to fight and inflict damage on the best ARVN units.

MANG YANG PASS

This battle was part of a Viet Cong (VC) operation in central Binh Dinh Province to cut Highway 19, the main supply route between the major port in the area (Qui Nhon) and the highlands region. If successful, it would have isolated the highland provinces of Kontum and Pleiku. Cut off from supplies by road, they would then depend only on aircraft for resupply. This would have further weakened morale and put the VC in an excellent position for a later offensive, during the rainy season, against Kontum and Pleiku.

Attack and counterattack

On February 20, the VC launched an all-out effort to seize Highway 19 and cut off the highlands. First they struck at an outpost of the Civilian Irregular Defense Group (CIDG), local civilians trained by U.S. Green Berets). This was Forward Operational Base No. 1 (FOB1), east of Mang Yang Pass. The CIDG forces at An Khe immediately sent reinforcements. As they approached the outpost they ran into an ambush, but launched an attack which caused the VC to retreat.

Plans were then made for a CIDG unit from Soui Doi, a camp west of Mang Yang Pass, to advance east down Highway 19 while the forces in An Khe would advance west. In this way the VC would be trapped between them.

However, the VC counterattacked, and soon a company of South Vietnamese Rangers and a company of CIDG soldiers, along with a U.S. Army Green Beret A-Team, were trapped near the Mang Yang Pass on Highway 19. General Westmoreland exercised the emergency authority which was granted to him by President Johnson in January for the use of U.S. jet aircraft. Twenty-four F-100 Super Sabres, with B-57 Canberra bombers and helicopter gunships, attacked the ambush site, while U.S. Army helicopters manage to evacuate the besieged South Vietnamese force without the loss of single man.

MANG YANG PASS

Location Binh Dinh Province

Date February 20-24, 1965

Commanders and forces Viet Cong; ARVN: 220 ARVN and CIDG troops (Colonel Hieu)

Casualties Viet Cong: 200 killed

Key actions The use of air power to support troops on the ground against the VC

Key effects Under procedures developed by the 2d Air Division, then commanded by Major-General Joseph Moore, the use of U.S. jet fighters in order to support the South Vietnamese Army when heavily engaged became standard practice afterward.

A machine-gun team engages the Viet Cong in the Mang Yang Pass area in early 1964.

PHU QUI DEPOT

U.S. naval leaders anticipated an intensification of the conflict in Southeast Asia in 1964. They therefore accelerated preparation of the fleet for the limited conventional war that national strategists had long studied as the logical response to localized aggression. During late 1964 and early 1965, 15 ships (one attack carrier, three submarines, 10 destroyers, and one assault ship) reinforced the Seventh Fleet in the Western Pacific.

Early in 1965 the Navy shifted passenger, cargo, and tanker ships to the Western Pacific, reactivated National Defense Reserve Fleet auxiliary ships, and chartered U.S. and foreign merchantmen to establish an efficient ocean transport system to Southeast Asia. The number of aircraft in the fleet replacement pool was doubled and a patrol squadron, equipped with Lockheed P-3 Orion aircraft, was relocated to the Western Pacific. The latest weapons, including improved Sidewinder and Sparrow air-to-air missiles, the new antiradar Shrike air-to-ground missile, and modernized 20mm cannon, were rushed to the fleet. Stocks of bombs, missiles, and other ordnance were increased and the replacement process improved.

The navy joins Rolling Thunder

The U.S. Navy did not delay in using its new weapons and aircraft. It joined Operation Rolling Thunder in March 1965, when 64 A-4 Skyhawks, A-1 Skyraiders, and 30 supporting aircraft from the Task Force 77 carriers USS *Hancock* and USS *Ranger* attacked the Phu Qui ammunition depot.

PHU QUI DEPOT

Location 100 miles (160 km) south of Hanoi, North Vietnam

Date March 15, 1965

Commanders and forces U.S. Navy: Task Force 77 (100 aircraft)

Casualties Unknown

Key actions This was the second set of raids in Operation Rolling Thunder and the first in which U.S. aircraft used napalm.

Key effects The operation reflected a key shift in U.S. strategic policy toward the war in Southeast Asia. It was no longer necessary that each air strike be a joint U.S.–South Vietnamese operation; that under no circumstances were actions to be taken that might result in air-to-air combat with North Vietnamese MiG fighters; that air operations were restricted below the 20th Parallel; or that Washington had final approval for alternate targets if local situations changed.

BATTLE OF VUNG TAU

Three Viet Cong fighters stand on top of an ARVN M113 armored personnel carrier they have knocked out.

Signaling an increase in the U.S. war effort, on May 15, 1965, the U.S. Army's 173rd Airborne Brigade carried out its first combat air assaults aboard 18 UH-1s flying in two airlifts. Between May 27 and 29, soldiers from the 173rd Airborne Brigade stationed at Vung Tau conducted a large-scale operation when intelligence reports confirmed the presence of the enemy. Elements of the 3rd Battalion, 319th Artillery Regiment, provided fire support for the paratroopers. For two days the 1st Battalion, 503rd Infantry Regiment, engaged the Viet Cong in a series of pitched battles. The Viet Cong broke off their contact with the Americans after suffering seven dead or wounded. The soldiers of the 173rd Airborne sufferd eight wounded.

BATTLE OF VUNG TAU

Location Bien Hoa, South Vietnam

Date May 27–29, 1965

Commanders and forces Viet Cong; U.S.: 173rd Airborne Brigade (Brigadier General Ellis W. Williamson)

Casualties Viet Cong: seven killed; U.S.: eight wounded

Key actions Upon arrival, one battalion of the Royal Australian Army and a battery from New Zealand were attached to the Brigade, making the 173d Airborne the only multinational combat unit in the war.

Key effects Deployed to Vietnam in May 1965, the brigade was the first major ground combat unit of the United States Army to serve there.

A U.S. M109 self-propelled howitzer, with ammunition alongside, stands ready to provide artillery support in War Zone D.

At the end of June 1965, General Westmoreland directed that the 173rd Airborne Brigade join with South Vietnamese units in a combined invasion of War Zone D, where a vast enemy stronghold was located.

The plan devised by General Ellis W. Williamson required his two U.S. battalions to conduct an airmobile assault into Landing Zone North, some 16 miles (25 km) north of Bien Hoa. Moving southward, the force would conduct a four-day search and destroy mission in the same area. At the same time, two South Vietnamese battalions would move into Helicopter Landing Zone (HLZ) South, about 3 miles (5 km) to the southwest of Landing Zone North, and remain in the field for about 24 hours in order to seek out enemy forces. Fire support came from the 173rd's artillery, located less than 1.2 miles (2 km) west of the landing zone.

The operation is launched

Elements of the South Vietnamese 48th Regiment, 10th ARVN Infantry Division, escorted the artillery and command post units to their positions. Remaining at Bien Hoa, Australian troops formed a reserve force ready to move at an hour's notice.

Following artillery and air bombardments, the American and South Vietnamese units deployed to their landing zones during the late morning and early afternoon of June 28. For the next two days they and the Australians combed their assigned areas for Viet Cong. They uncovered many stores of ammunition and weapons, over 200 tons (203 tonnes) of rice, and large quantities of dried milk, tea, corn, barley, and tobacco. Except for scattered sniping and a few mortar rounds directed at the American and Allied troops, the enemy kept its distance.

INTO WAR ZONE D

Location War Zone D, 20 miles (32 km) north of Saigon, South Vietnam

Date June 28–30, 1965

Commanders and forces Viet Cong; U.S.: 173rd Airborne Brigade; ARVN: 10th Infantry Division

Casualties Unknown

Key actions Although the operation ended with little enemy contact, it nonetheless represented a number of "firsts" in the war in Vietnam for the U.S. forces involved. Involving over 140 UH-1s, flying several sorties each to transport the two U.S. and two South Vietnamese battalions to their targets, the attack was not only the largest troop helicopter lift to date, but also the first major ground combat operation conducted by U.S. forces in the Vietnam War

Key effects As a test of cooperation between U.S. and ARVN forces, it was a resounding success.

Throughout July 1965 evidence pointed to a Viet Cong (VC) buildup south of Chu Lai, a base 56 miles (90 km) southeast of Da Nang. Operation Starlite was designed to destroy the 1st VC Regiment in the area. The terrain was dominated by sandy flats, broken by numerous streams and an occasional wooded knoll. The scattered hamlets possessed paddy areas and dry fields.

The American attack force was under the command of the 7th Marines and consisted of the 2d Battalion, 4th Marine Regiment, and the 3rd Battalion, 3rd Marine Regiment, from Chu Lai, and the 1st and 3rd Battalions of the 7th Marine Regiment from the Special Landing Force. Starlite began on August 18, 1965, with U.S. Marines leading the dawn attack. The 3rd Battalion, 7th Marine Regiment, landed by helicopter and across the beach later that day. The 7th Marine Regiment joined the operation on August 20.

The three-pronged attack combined a river crossing in LVTP-5s (Landing Vehicle Tanks, Personnel) from the north, a helicopter assault in the west, and an amphibious landing on the southeast beach of the Van Tuong Peninsula. The Marines were hit by intense mortar and rifle fire and suffered five dead and 17 wounded. They called in artillery and air support to knock out the mortar and automatic fire. When they finally attacked they found the VC unit had fled, though pockets of resistance continued from other VC soldiers holed up in bunkers and caves.

Piranha was a search and destroy follow-up to Operation Starlite aimed at the remnants of what was left of the 1st VC Regiment. Some 40 UH-34D helicopters were used to transport the 1st Battalion, 7th Marine Regiment, into Landing Zone Oak, 4 miles (6.4 km) inland from the amphibious landing of another battalion. This assault took three hours. Then, 16 UH-34D helicopters went to Quang Ngai and began shuttling two South Vietnamese battalions into Landing Zones Birch and Pine, escorted by four army gunships. At these landing zones, the U.S. Marine helicopters came under light small-arms fire. During the 12-day operation the Marines again worked well with ARVN forces.

OPERATION PIRANHA

Location Quang Ngai Province, South Vietnam

Date September 7–19, 1965

Commanders and forces Viet Cong: 1st Regiment; U.S.: 7th Marine Regiment; ARVN: 4th Regiment

Casualties Viet Cong: 183 killed, 360 taken prisoner; U.S.: 2 killed, 14 wounded; ARVN: 5 killed, 33 wounded

Key actions The 3rd Battalion, 7th Marine Regiment, was helilifted to its objective, encountered no opposition, and completed the helilift in less than three hours.

Key effects Considering the magnitude of the effort, the operation could hardly be called a success. Local villagers told the Marines that units of the target 1st VC Regiment had been in the area, but they left less than 24 hours before Operation Piranha started. The operation did nothing to give the local population confidence in U.S. and ARVN forces.

OPERATION STARLITE

Location Quang Ngai Province, South Vietnam

Date August 18–24, 1965

Commanders and forces Viet Cong: 1st Regiment; U.S.: 2d Battalion, 4th Marine Regiment, 3rd Battalion, 3rd Marine Regiment, 1st and 3rd Battalions, 7th Marine Regiment

Casualties Viet Cong: 964 killed; U.S.: 45 killed, 203 wounded

Key actions The use of Marine artillery and air support to suppress VC mortar and automatic fire.

Key effects This operation frustrated an enemy attack against the Marine base at Chu Lai, and also rendered the 1st Viet Cong Regiment ineffective. A more permanent result was that the Viet Cong discovered that they could not defeat the Marines in a stand-up battle. This offensive likewise forced the Viet Cong away from their bases along the coastline, where they had previously found sanctuary from their enemies.

U.S. Marines and an M113 armored personnel carrier near Da Nang in mid-1965.

A battalion from the 1st Brigade, 101st Airborne Division, began landing in the rugged Song Con Valley, 18 miles (29 km) northeast of An Khe. The American troops encountered heavy enemy fire at the landing zone. Four helicopters were lost and their company commanders killed. Reinforcements could not land because of the intensity of the enemy fire. In the fight at close quarters, the Americans were unable to call in close air support, armed gunships, and artillery fire without endangering their own lives. But as the enemy pressed them back, supporting artillery fire was placed right on top of the enemy. By dusk the fighting died down as the paratroopers prepared for a night attack. The Viet Cong, hard hit by about 100 air strikes and 11,000 rounds of artillery, began to slip away. Inspection of the battlefield the next day revealed that the Americans had landed in the midst of a heavily bunkered enemy base.

SONG CON VALLEY

Location Song Con Valley, South Vietnam

Date September 17–18, 1965

Commanders and forces Viet Cong; U.S.: 1st Brigade, 101st Airborne Division

Casualties Unknown

Key actions The intensity of the Viet Cong (VC) gunfire halted the operation almost immediately. But the VC underestimated the willingness of U.S. commanders to call in air and artillery support when fighting at close quarters.

Key effects The fight at Song Con Valley was significant in that it had many of the hallmarks of the highland battles that were to come. Americans had little intelligence on either the enemy or the area of operation. The Viet Cong employed for the first time the "hugging" tactics that prevented Americans from employing either close-in air support or artillery fire without endangering themselves.

Realizing that time was working against him, General Vo Nguyen Giap, commander of the North Vietnamese Army (NVA), sent three regiments south to the Central Highlands of South Vietnam. (The five provinces of the Central Highlands—Kontum, Gia Lai, Dak Lak, Dak Nong, and Lam Dong—stretched along the high ridge of the Trong Son mountain range of the Annamese Cordillera that serves as a natural border between Vietnam and Laos and Cambodia.) Their mission was to split South Vietnam in two before the Americans built up their strength.

Desperate defense at Plei Mei

The U.S. Special Forces Camp at Plei Mei came under heavy attacks from the 33rd NVA Regiment all through the night of October 19 and into the next day. The CIDG forces fought desperately, but the enemy took part of the camp. A Nung force and ARVN Rangers were sent to strengthen the camp. If Plei Mei fell, Pleiku, key to the Central Highlands, would be next.

In response to the NVA incursion into the Central Highlands, a force of armor and infantry from the Army of the Republic of South Vietnam was ordered to relieve the beleaguered Plei Mei camp. When he ran into an ambush on Highway 5, south of Pleiku, on October 23, the South Vietnamese major leading the force began to hesitate. It took his troops another two days to travel less than 20 miles (32 km). When it got to within 4 miles (6.4 km) of the camp, the armored column was hit by another ambush by elements of the 33rd NVA Regiment. Despite the failure of the relief force to get there, however, the camp at Plei Mei did not fall and the NVA regiment was beaten off.

ATTACK ON PLEI MEI

Location Pleiku Province, South Vietnam

Date October 19–25, 1965

Commanders and forces NVA: 33rd Regiment; U.S.: Green Berets Detachment A-217 (Captain Moore), CIDG forces

Casualties Unknown

Key actions As would be seen often in the war, the ARVN soldiers, even with good equipment, performed poorly.

Key effects The U.S. 1st Air Cavalry Division (Airmobile) was deployed into the area. This would result in the Battle of Ia Drang.

BATTLE OF IA DRANG

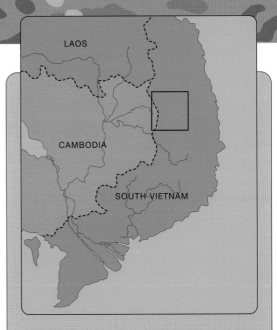

This engagement was one of the first major battles between the United States Army and the North Vietnamese Army (NVA) during the Vietnam War. As the U.S. 1st Cavalry Division (Airmobile) began the second stage of General Westmoreland's search-and-destroy mission, enemy forces began to move out of their bases in the Chu Pong Massif, mountains near the Cambodian border. Units of the 1st Cavalry Division advanced to establish artillery bases and landing zones at the base of the Chu Pong Massif.

Landing Zone X-Ray was one of several U.S. positions which remained vulnerable to attack by enemy forces occupying the surrounding high ground. Fighting began on November 14, pitting three U.S. Army battalions against elements of two NVA regiments. Withstanding repeated mortar attacks and infantry assaults, the American troops used all means of firepower at their disposal, including the division's own gunships, massive artillery bombardments, hundreds of bombing and strafing attacks by tactical aircraft, and earth-shattering "arc light" strikes by B-52 Stratofortress bombers based on Guam, and eventually turned back the determined enemy.

Desperate defense at Plei Mei

Although badly mauled, the NVA did not retreat. Elements of the 66th North Vietnamese Regiment moved east toward Plei Mei and encountered an American battalion on November 17, a few miles north of Landing Zone X-Ray. The fight that resulted was a stark reminder of the North Vietnamese mastery of the ambush. The communists quickly trapped three U.S. Army infantry battalions. As the trapped units struggled to fight their way out, nearly all semblance of organized combat disappeared. Neither reinforcements nor firepower could be brought in. Combat was reduced to hand-to-hand and small-unit fighting.

When the fighting ended, 60 percent of the Americans were casualties, with one of every three soldiers in the battalions engaged killed or wounded. Notwithstanding the many problems associated with the fighting in the Ia Drang Valley, however, Westmoreland and his staff expressed satisfaction with what was the first major U.S. victory of the war.

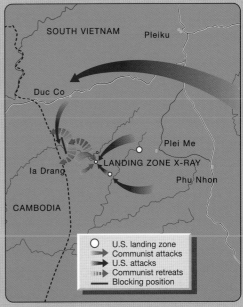

U.S. landing zone
Communist attacks
U.S. attacks
Communist retreats
Blocking position

BATTLE OF IA DRANG

Location	Ia Drang Valley, South Vietnam
Date	November 14–18, 1965
Commanders and forces	NVA: 32d, 33rd, and 66th Regiments—4,000 troops (Nguyen Huu An); U.S.: 1st Battalion, 7th Cavalry—1,000 troops (Lieutenant Colonel Hal Moore)
Casualties	NVA: 1,519 killed; U.S.: 79 killed, 121 wounded

Key actions In a head- to-head clash, an outnumbered U.S. force had spoiled an enemy operation and sent a major NVA force reeling back in defeat, inflicting far more casualties than it sustained.

Key effects The battle in the Ia Drang Valley had important implications for the future conduct of the war. The army favored "search and destroy" missions, such as the Ia Drang operation, designed to bring the NVA to battle and then to destroy it. Although U.S. casualties were high, estimated NVA casualties were far higher. Thus the Pleiku campaign convinced General Westmoreland that his "search and destroy" concept was correct.

OPERATION SILVER BAYONET

Following the clash at the Plei Mei Special Forces camp, 30 miles (48 km) southwest of Pleiku, earlier in the month, the U.S. 1st Cavalry Division (Airmobile) launched Operation Silver Bayonet in October 1965. It was designed to provide security and artillery support to ARVN forces around Plei Mei. The operational area totaled 2,500 square miles (6,475 square km) of thick jungle. The 1st Cavalry Division was ideally suited for this, as it had 400 helicopters to transport its soldiers. U.S. troops, in conjunction with South Vietnamese forces, sought to destroy North Vietnamese forces operating in Pleiku Province in II Corps Tactical Zone (the Central Highlands). The operation concluded in November with a week of bitter fighting when fleeing North Vietnamese troops decided to protect an important staging area and supply base in the Ia Drang Valley (see page 21). In an associated engagement, 500 North Vietnamese soldiers ambushed another battalion from the 1st Cavalry Division at Landing

Zone Albany, wiping out almost an entire company. Reported enemy casualties for the month-long Operation Silver Bayonet totaled 1,771 enemy soldiers. But the Americans had certainly not destroyed the NVA's ability to wage war.

OPERATION SILVER BAYONET

Location   Pleiku Province, South Vietnam

Date   October 23–November 20, 1965

Commanders and forces   NVA: 33rd and 66th Regiments; U.S.: 1st Cavalry Division (Airmobile)

Casualties   NVA: 1,771 killed and wounded; U.S.: 200 killed and wounded

Key actions   On November 14, after the 3rd Brigade of the 1st Cavalry Division had relieved the 1st Brigade in the vicinity of Plei Mei and Pleiku, the most significant phase of Silver Bayonet began. Airmobile search and destroy operations were initiated, which resulted in very heavy and intense contacts with NVA forces.

Key effects   After seeing the determination of NVA units the American command in Vietnam concluded that only a substantial increase in U.S. military aid could ensure the South's survival.

UH-1 Huey helicopters of the U.S. 1st Cavalry Division during Operation Silver Bayonet. Each Huey could carry up to 11 troops.

OPERATION BLOODHOUND

Two U.S. Army infantry battalions, including the 2d Battalion of the 2d Infantry Regiment, moved to Landing Zone Dallas inside the Michelin Rubber Plantation in Binh Duong Province on December 1. The site functioned as a staging base for the two infantry battalions for their search and destroy mission and also acted as a command post for the brigade.

On December 2, Colonel William D. Brodbeck's 3rd Brigade of the 1st Infantry Division's task force searched toward the southeast of Landing Zone Dallas in a rectangle-sized area of heavy undergrowth that extended for about 8 miles (13 km) west to east, and 12 miles (20 km) to the south. Two infantry battalions maneuvered methodically over several days from phase line to phase line in search of the elusive enemy, but failed to find the Viet Cong (VC).

On December 5, Lieutenant Colonel George M. Shuffer's 2d Battalion of the 2d Infantry Regiment finally made contact with the Viet Cong. The battalion began the day searching along a jungle road in a southerly direction. At midday, just north of the hamlet of Nha Mat and 5 miles (9 km) west of Bau Bang, Shuffer's lead troops came under small-arms, mortar, machine-gun, and artillery rifle fire from the surrounding trees. The encounter soon turned into a major firefight, and was only resolved when artillery from the 1st Division's 175mm self-propelled guns laid down heavy fire. Eventually, the Viet Cong broke off the firefight and abandoned the battlefield, leaving their dead, weapons, and equipment behind.

OPERATION BLOODHOUND

Location Binh Duong Province, South Vietnam

Date December 1–9, 1965

Commanders and forces Viet Cong; U.S.: 3rd Brigade, 1st Infantry Division, 502d Airborne Battalion, 101st Airborne Division

Casualties Viet Cong: 550 killed and wounded; U.S.: 200 killed and wounded

Key actions As the Viet Cong tried to "hug" the American troops by moving in close, Shuffer's troops maintained a heavy volume of fire, keeping them at a distance. This allowed the 1st Infantry Division's artillery to bombard the VC forces.

Key effects The operation once again showed the effectiveness of air power, the Americans flying 109 close air sorties over nine days.

OPERATION SMASH I

U.S helicopters land troops during the search for the Viet Cong in Operation Smash I at the end of 1965.

Operation Smash I started when paratroopers of the 173rd Airborne Brigade move into position west of Highway 15, Bien Hoa Province. The operation began in this way in order to deter an enemy attack, which was expected near Saigon during the Christmas truce.

Lieutenant Colonel George E. Dexter, leading the 2d Battalion of the 503rd Infantry Regiment, soon found the enemy. On December 18, operating from the battalion's base, the 2d Battalion carried out two company sized search-and-destroy operations to the northeast and west. Shortly after 10:30 hours, and only about 0.3 miles (0.5 km) from the base camp, the company which was operating to the northeast stumbled upon the dug-in Viet Cong.

When the Viet Cong opened up with machine-gun and antitank fire, the company under Lieutenant-Colonel Dexter returned fire and also called in artillery and air support. The Viet Cong broke off the attack and left behind their dead and numerous small arms and ammunition scattered over the battlefield. Lieutenant Colonel Dexter's force losses were light.

OPERATION SMASH I

Location Bien Hoa Province, South Vietnam

Date December 17–21, 1965

Commanders and forces Viet Cong; U.S.: 2d Battalion, 503rd Infantry Regiment (Lieutenant Colonel George E. Dexter)

Casualties Viet Cong: 62 killed; U.S.: 6 killed

Key actions U.S. Air Force F-105 Thunderchiefs and F-4 Phantom jets flew 14 close air support sorties, and U.S. artillery fired a total of 1,000 rounds at the Viet Cong positions.

Key effects Once again American air power had proved decisive against the Viet Cong.

By 1966, the war in Vietnam had become "America's War." Soldiers, sailors, Marines, and airmen now engaged in battle with the Viet Cong and, for the first time, elements of the North Vietnamese Army (NVA). General Westmoreland's strategy of conducting large search-and-destroy missions resulted in drawing both the Viet Cong and the NVA into battle. As the 1st Cavalry Division had demonstrated in the Battle of the Ia Drang Valley, like the 173rd Airborne Brigade's combat operations in the Central Highlands and the 1st Infantry Division's actions in III Corps Tactical Zone, the Viet Cong and North Vietnamese could not match U.S. firepower or maneuverability—once the enemy could be found. As the U.S. Army sent more units to South Vietnam, the rate of inflicted casualties on the enemy increased rapidly, but it did not stop the flow of men and material from North Vietnam from entering South Vietnam via the infamous Ho Chi Minh Trail. However, the U.S. Army proved that it still was the master of the battlefield when it cornered the Viet Cong and NVA.

Unfortunately for Westmoreland, search-and-destroy, though an aggressive tactic, was a failure. It was the communists who usually initiated fighting, invariably at a time and place of their choosing, and broke off combat when they saw fit. In addition, 200,000 North Vietnamese males reached draft age every year. Westmoreland's aim of wearing down the enemy through attrition was never likely to succeed.

U.S. Air Force operations

As the year progressed, the U.S. Air Force's (USAF's) Operation Rolling Thunder, the sustained bombing of North Vietnam and targets in South Vietnam and along the South Vietnamese–Laotian border, increased in tempo and intensity. USAF B-52 Stratofortress bombers, based primarily on the island of Guam, likewise increased their assistance to tactical air strikes in South Vietnam against enemy ground targets in "arc light"

American troops rest on a sand-bagged bunker in South Vietnam. The soldier in the foreground is armed with an M79 grenade launcher, a weapon often used in jungle firefights.

missions. F-105 Thunderchiefs and F-4B Phantom jets, from bases in Thailand and South Vietnam, pummelled North Vietnamese and Viet Cong positions with 250lb and 500lb bombs. U.S. Navy jets and their Air Force and U.S. Marine counterparts flew tactical and strategic air strikes off the aircraft carriers on "Yankee Station."

The U.S. Navy

The U.S. Navy and its South Vietnamese allies patrolled the many rivers and waterways in southern Vietnam and along that country's long coastline. Operation Market Time (a combined U.S. Navy and South Vietnamese Navy effort to stop the flow of supplies from North Vietnam) began to have an effect on the flow of weapons and men reaching the Viet Cong operating in the Mekong Delta in the south. The "Seabees" of the Naval Construction Battalions undertook major civic missions, as well as military construction projects. Navy doctors, nurses, and corpsmen brought their healing skills to U.S. Marines and soldiers, as well as ARVN and other Free World troops, and gave Allied troops possibly the best medical care ever provided to soldiers in the field. Also, members of the U.S. Coast Guard provided harbor and port defense and management, as well as staging patrols with their U.S. Navy counterparts.

A well-armed enemy

The year 1966 witnessed a tenfold increase in activity for the U.S. military as it faced a brave and determined enemy. By mid-1966, American troops found themselves fighting North Vietnamese Army troops equipped with the AK-47 Kalashnikov assault rifle and RP-2s (rocket-propeled grenade launchers) in ever-increasing numbers. By the end of 1966 enemy units were employing superior Soviet-supplied weapons. Viet Cong and NVA sappers launched heavy mortar attacks against the Special Forces camp at Khe Sanh and the Da Nang airfield. In addition, Soviet 120mm heavy mortars allowed the communists to launch attacks against other major U.S. military installations throughout the South and thereby increase the problems of base security.

The 173rd Airborne Brigade was ordered to locate and destroy the 506th Viet Cong (VC) Local Force Battalion, reported by intelligence sources to be near Bao Trai in the Mekong Delta. The 506th Battalion had been operating with relative impunity in the area for a year or more. In addition, units of the 267th VC Main Force Battalion of the Dong Thap Regiment were said to be passing through the area.

All the American units involved in the operation reported mobility problems because many of the rice paddies and sugar cane fields in the area were flooded. Crisscrossing the area were numerous streams and canals, with a lot of silt on the bottoms.

Many unoccupied VC bunkers were discovered in the dikes bordering the canals and paddies. The bunkers possessed good fields of fire. An article on Operation Marauder in the January 5, 1966, issue of *The New York*

A U.S. Skyraider drops a phosphorus bomb on a target. Phosphorus is very damaging to the skin since it burns fiercely.

Times provided a good description of the setting and gave some idea of how difficult search-and-destroy operations were in the area: "The gloomy and dismal Plain of Reeds is full of chest-deep canals, standing water, and fetid, nauseating, smelly mud." Small forested patches and villages were interspersed among the canals and watery fields.

The New York Times also summarized the battle: "For eight hours the Americans crouched in the muck behind paddy dikes and watched bombs, napalm, artillery, and mortar shells hit the enemy."

During the operation U.S. troops apprehended numerous VC suspects. They also questioned residents of the area, who told them that the 506th Local Battalion had long been operating throughout the sector. They noted, however, that in the past several days they had seen elements of the 506th breaking down into small groups and leaving the area.

OPERATION MARAUDER

Location Plain of Reeds, Mekong Delta

Date January 1–6, 1966

Commanders and forces Viet Cong: 267th Main Force Battalion, 506th Local Force Battalion; U.S.: 173rd Airborne Brigade (Brigadier General Ellis Williamson)

Casualties Viet Cong: 100 killed; U.S.: unknown

Key actions Air strikes and artillery bombardments shattered Viet Cong resistance.

Key effects The Viet Cong 267th Main Force Battalion was routed.

OPERATION CRIMP

CAMBODIA

Plain of Reeds

Chan Phu •Moc Hoa Saigon
Mekong Ap Bac Nha Be
Long Xuyen Dong Tam My Tho
Sadec Ben Tri
Vinh Long
Can Tho

Kanh Hung Long Phu

Bac Lieu

Ca Mau

SOUTH CHINA SEA

THE MEKONG DELTA

General Westmoreland launched Operation Crimp with the 173rd Airborne Brigade and other elements of the 1st Division. General Williamson's mission was to hunt down and destroy the Viet Cong's headquarters for the Saigon area. As B-52 Stratofortress bombers' preparatory strikes "softened" up the Ho Bo Woods, Colonel Brodbeck's 3rd Brigade command group and support elements reached Trung Lap, located on the western edge of the area of operations.

In the meantime, two of the three maneuver battalions deployed by helicopter to the southwest corner of the objective. One battalion blocked off the south side of the woods, while the other searched for the enemy. The third battalion moved by truck from Di An to Trang Lap and then moved on foot to the sector of the sweeping action to which it had been assigned. But the Viet Cong had already left.

OPERATION CRIMP

Location Tay Ninh Province, South Vietnam

Date January 7–11, 1966

Commanders and forces Viet Cong: Military Region 4; US: 1st Infantry Division, 173d Airborne Brigade, and the Royal Australian Regiment (8,000 troops in all)

Casualties Viet Cong: 218 killed; U.S.: 6 killed, 45 wounded

Key actions Crimp failed to find and destroy or capture personnel, equipment, and intelligence material of the Viet Cong headquarters.

Key effects Operation Crimp and its successor, Operation Mastiff (February 1966), served as frustrating reminders to the U.S. commanders that the Viet Cong was able to avoid battle with large formations if it so desired.

OPERATION VAN BUREN

UH-1H Huey helicopters of the U.S. 101st Airborne Division in South Vietnam in early 1966.

The 1st Brigade, 101st Airborne Division, along with the South Korean 2d Marine Brigade and the ARVN 47th Regiment, launched Operation Van Buren to locate and destroy the North Vietnamese Army's (NVA's) 95th Regiment in the Tuy Hoa Valley, and to protect the important rice harvest in the coastal region. During the operation a South Korean platoon of about 13 men wiped out an elite North Vietnamese Army regiment. There were only two Koreans lost and more than 400 NVA soldiers killed. It began as a gun battle but broke down into hand-to-hand combat. The Allied forces that fought to aid South Vietnam were called "Free World Military Forces" by President Johnson. Of these forces, the troops of the Republic of Korea (ROK) were some of the best soldiers fighting the communists.

OPERATION VAN BUREN

Location Phu Yen Province, South Vietnam

Date January 20–February 20, 1966

Commanders and forces NVA: 95th Regiment; Free World: U.S. 101st Airborne Division. ROK 2d Marine Brigade, ARVN 47th Regiment

Casualties NVA: 679 killed; U.S.: 55 killed, 221 wounded

Key actions More than 30,000 tons (30,480 tonnes) of harvested rice were secured.

Key effects The success of this major combined operation was measured from the 679 enemy soldiers killed, 49 captured, and 177 who defected to the Americans and Koreans, as well as to the South Vietnamese.

OPERATION MASHER

U.S. troops race from their helicopter during Operation Masher. The Viet Cong often swept helicopter landing zones with gunfire.

Four battalions of the U.S. Army 1st Cavalry Division began Operation Masher near Bong Son in the coastal region of Binh Dinh Province, 53 miles (85 km) north of Qui Nhon. The purpose of the operation was to drive the North Vietnamese out of the province and destroy enemy supply areas. Six battalions of ARVN airborne and six ARVN infantry battalions from the 22d ARVN Division (Reinforced), an airmobile division, began Operation Thang Phong II, the South Vietnamese companion operation to Masher, in Binh Dinh Province. The name of the operation was later changed from Operation Masher to White Wing at the insistence of President Johnson. Masher was the largest search-and-destroy mission up to that point in the war, but critics argued that the massive amount of firepower used had resulted in too few enemy casualties.

OPERATION MASHER

Location Binh Dinh Province, South Vietnam

Date January 24–March 6, 1966

Commanders and forces NVA: 18th & 19th Regiments, VC: 1st& 2d Regiments; Free World: U.S. 1st Cavalry Division, ARVN I and II Corps

Casualties NVA: 1,342 killed; U.S.: 288 killed, 990 wounded; ARVN: 808 killed

Key actions Helicopters lifted entire infantry battalions a total of 78 times and moved artillery batteries 55 times.

Key effects The U.S. Government summarized the amount of firepower deployed during Operation Masher/White wing as follows: 1,352 strikes coupled with 1,126 fighter sorties unloaded 1.5 million lb (682,000 kg) of bombs and 292,000 lb (132,700 kg) of napalm. But Masher caused a major increase in Vietnamese refugees.

OPERATION UTAH

Operation Utah/Lien Kiet 26 began as a combined operation of the U.S. Marines and ARVN in the vicinity of Quang Ngai City against North Vietnamese Army (NVA) and Viet Cong (VC) forces. Marine helicopters, covered by Marine Corps close air support, took the 1st ARVN Airborne Battalion to a point southeast of Chau Nhai (3), a hamlet in South Vietnam that bore the same name as two others and was numbered for convenience. The landing zone was hot with enemy gunfire and a Marine F-4 Phantom jet was shot down. But the Vietnamese battalions landed and went immediately into the attack in good order. It was followed mid-morning by the 2d Battalion, 7th Marine Regiment, which moved into the ARVN's right flank, while in the mid-afternoon the 3rd Battalion, 1st Marine Regiment, landed north of the action. The 2d ARVN Division also put in additional battalions. The last opening in the ring was closed the next day by the 2d Battalion, 4th Marine Regiment, landing to the south and cutting off any enemy escape. Finally, the Task Force Reserve made up of the 1st Battalion, 7th Marine Regiment, and a company of ARVN scouts took up blocking positions 3.7 miles (6 km) southwest of Binh Son. Most of the action was over by dawn of March 6 after a short, hard fight.

OPERATION UTAH

Location Quang Ngai, South Vietnam

Date March 4–8, 1966

Commanders and forces NVA and Viet Cong; Free World: U.S. 7th Marine Regiment, 2d ARVN Division;

Casualties NVA: 600 Killed; U.S.: 98 killed, 278 wounded; ARVN: 30 killed, 120 wounded

Key actions The NVA used several 12.7mm antiaircraft weapons to oppose the helicopter assaults although the ground units initially received only light resistance. Both the ARVN and the Marines added more infantry and artillery units. There were several major battles. Artillery and air strikes were used on a continuous basis. On March 5, the NVA struck the ARVN near Hill 50 around 05:00 hours. Marine Corps artillery fired 1,900 rounds in support for two hours.

Key effects This was the first U.S. Marine contact with the NVA.

ATTACK ON A SHAU

The A Shau CIDG camp had the primary mission of border surveillance and attacking enemy infiltration routes into its assigned area of operation. The camp was located southwest of Hue and approximately 3 miles (5 km) east of the Laotian border. The camp consisted of some barracks buildings, a triangular fort, and an airstrip made of pierced steel planking. The fort had a mortar bunker at each corner. The walls consisted of steel plate and sandbags. The airstrip was east of the camp, outside the barbed wire perimeter.

On the evening of March 8, the camp's strength was as follows: 10 U.S. Green Berets, 210 CIDG, 141 Mike Force (highly trained locals), 9 interpreters, and 41 civilians.

At 03:50 hours on March 9 the camp began receiving heavy 81mm mortar fire which continued until 06:30 hours. A probe by two North Vietnamese Army (NVA) companies began on the south wall at approximately 04:30 hours. They were met with heavy fire and fell back. The initial barrage of NVA mortar fire was extremely accurate. It caused heavy damage to supply huts and water storage and contributed to the temporary loss of radio communications with the outside world.

At 04:00 hours on March 10 the camp again began receiving intense and extremely accurate mortar fire. In addition, NVA 57mm artillery rifle fire reduced almost all the remaining buildings to rubble. This heavy fire continued throughout the entire day in varying intensity, until the camp was eventually evacuated by the Americans at 17:30 hours.

ATTACK ON A SHAU

Location   Thua Thien Province, South Vietnam

Date   March 9–10, 1966

Commanders and forces   NVA: 325th Division; Free World: 10 U.S. Green Berets, 210 South Vietnamese Civilian Irregular Defense Group (CIDG), 141 Mike Force

Casualties   NVA: 800 killed (estimate); U.S: 8 killed, 12 wounded, 5 missing; South Vietnamese: 47 killed or missing

Key actions   The NVA attack took full advantage of bad weather conditions to hinder tactical air support, reinforcement, and resupply attempts by the U.S. Air Force.

Key effects   It was two years before Allied forces retook the valley. The NVA established its own camp at A Shau, ringed the valley with anti-aircraft batteries, and used it as a staging area and a supply dump.

US Marines exit a CH-46 Sea Knight under enemy fire. The CH-46 was purchased in 1964 to meet the troop-lift requirements of the Marines in Vietnam.

This was a search-and-destroy operation conducted by a battalion-sized U.S. Marine force. Operation Georgia started as Lieutenant Colonel William W. Taylor's 3rd Battalion, 9th Marine Regiment, moved out toward An Hoa. Two rifle companies, supported by a platoon of armored vehicles, moved overland toward the objective area. These vehicles were fitted with a two-man turret with a 105mm howitzer, a 7.62mm machine gun, and .5in antiaircraft machine gun. They could also transport troops: In an emergency, they could carry up to 45 standing Marines. A third company arrived at An Hoa by helicopter, while U.S. Air Force transport aircraft brought in some 105mm howitzers to provide artillery support. Both fixed-wing transports and helicopters continued to fly in supplies for the An Hoa build-up during the day.

Attacking the Viet Cong

With the establishment of the An Hoa base, the Marines began the second phase of the operation. Lieutenant Colonel Taylor divided up his Marines, with local ARVN Forces, and launched them in a series of actions in order to secure the hamlets around the An Hoa base. Despite intelligence reports that the Viet Cong's 5th Battalion was in the area, the Marines encountered little opposition through the end of April, generally only harassing fire and mines.

In December 1966 the 3d Brigade Task Force, 25th Infantry Division, completed Operation Paul Revere through phase IV, setting the U.S. Army record for the longest sustained combat operation.

During the operation, four major battles and countless skirmishes were fought. The "Big Four" were: The Battle of Alpha 10 (May 29–30), involving elements of the 35th Infantry Regiment; the New Battle of Ia Drang (July 31–August 2), involving the same elements on a larger scale; the defensive battle of August 9, in which Americans and South Koreans fought off a North Vietnamese Army (NVA) Regiment; and the Battle for Dragon Crater on November 19, where the 1st Battalion, 14th Infantry Regiment, fought an NVA Regiment.

OPERATION PAUL REVERE I–IV

Location   Pleiku Province, South Vietnam

Date   May 10–December 31, 1966

Commanders and forces   NVA: unknown; U.S.: 25th Infantry Division

Casualties   NVA: 1,496 killed, 424 captured; U.S.: 313 killed

Key actions   The technique of "checkerboarding" (moving from one numbered 10,000-meter grid square to another), which had proved effective during previous operations, was continued.

Key effects   The biggest achievement of Paul Revere in the civic action field was the freeing of some 400 Montagnards who had been enslaved by the Viet Cong in 1962 and forced to grow rice and transport supplies for the NVA ever since.

A phosphorus bomb explodes in Operation Georgia. White phosphorus caused casualties and was also a good target marker.

OPERATION GEORGIA

Location   Quang Nam Province, South Vietnam

Date   April 21–May 10, 1966

Commanders and forces   VC: 5th Battalion, elite R-20 Battalion; U.S.: 9th Marine Regiment

Casualties   VC: 103 killed; U.S.: 9 killed, 94 wounded

Key actions   The heaviest action of Operation Georgia occurred when Captain George R. Griggs' M Company, 3rd Battalion, 9th Marines, which had only recently relieved another company during the operation, prepared to cross the Thu Bon. Its objective was the hamlet of Phu Long (1) on the northern bank of the river in the north-central sector of the Georgia area. While Captain Griggs' company crossed the river, an enemy force, the elite Viet Cong R-20 Battalion, opened fire on the Marine company. Reinforced by two Marine rifle companies and supported by air and artillery, the Marines captured Phu Long (1).

Key effects   The operation showed the value of having armored vehicles supporting infantry. In Georgia they were instrumental in neutralizing enemy fire and preventing more casualties.

In **Operation El Paso** the U.S. Army's 1st Infantry Division and the 5th ARVN Division engaged in combat against the Viet Cong 9th Main Division in Binh Long Province. During Operation El Paso a battalion commander and his small mobile command group embarked in three Ontos—fully tracked and lightly armed mobile carriers mounting six 106mm recoilless rifles and four .5in spotting rifles, as well as one .3in machine gun. Each vehicle had a crew of three. The Ontos was the main weapon of the Marine antitank battalion. But the Ontos found themselves stalled on the northern fringes of Phong Ho (2), a hamlet 6.2 miles (10 km) south of the Marble Mountain Air Facility, in an area which was noted for its hostility toward the government of South Vietnam. The Viet Cong opened up with a hail of small-arms fire. Using his command group with its Ontos as a blocking unit, the American commander ordered up reinforcements. They arrived supported by amphibious armored vehicles and tanks, brought up from the south of Phong Ho (2). The result was a sound defeat of the Viet Cong by the U.S. Marines, after which it was discovered that a total of 11 enemy soldiers had been killed and left on the battlefield. The operation continued into July, and resulted in hundreds of communist dead.

A U.S. soldier armed with an M60 machine gun. A machine-gun section was made up of a gunner, assistant gunner, and the ammunition carrier. The M60 can fire up to 550 rounds a minute.

OPERATION EL PASO

Location Binh Long Province, South Vietnam

Date June 2–July 13, 1966

Commanders and forces NVA: 9th Division; Free World: U.S. Army 1st Infantry Division, 5th ARVN Division

Casualties NVA: 855 dead; U.S.: 200 killed and wounded

Key actions The Battle of Ap Tau O was fought on the afternoon of June 8, 1966, 85 miles (136 km) north of Saigon, just south of Quan Loi and Hon Quan on National Highway 13. As the American troops were moving north on Highway 13, an air observer flying over the convoy spotted Viet Cong guerrillas along the road. The Americans immediately engaged the enemy. It was 14:40 hours and the U.S. unit had run into what was later identified as the 272d Main Force VC Regiment, three battalions strong. This battle occurred during the 1st Infantry Division's Operation El Paso.

Key effects Once again the communists showed their superior tactics. After the actual ambush, for example, or whenever the commander had decided the time had come, they would clear the battlefield quickly. They would carry off anything in the way of weapons, ammunition, and supplies that might be useful in the future, destroying what they could not carry. Finally, they would also carry off their dead and wounded. In mid-1966 it was clear that the Americans in South Vietnam had yet to devise a consistently successful way of dealing with such attacks. The experience gained in El Paso in June and July 1966 would provide some minor improvement. El Paso was also considered a success because Route 13 was reopened and secured. The use of armored vehicles again proved invaluable.

In early 1966, U.S. leaders concluded that the growing Allied strength in coastal areas would keep the enemy from concentrating large units there in the future. Amphibious raids and sweeps along the shore were no longer considered useful operations. From June through September, therefore, in a series of operations called Deckhouse, the U.S. Navy joined Army and U.S. Marine troops in combat actions inland.

U.S. Marine forces launched Operation Deckhouse I, the first in a series of operations conducted by the Special Landing Force (SLF) on Viet Cong coastal strongholds, on June 18. Marines conducted this operation in the Phu Yen Province, 12 miles (19.3 km) northwest of Tuy Hoa.

On July 16, Deckhouse II was carried out in the Dong Ha area by the so-called Ready Amphibious Force to permit the U.S. Seventh Fleet's Special Landing Force and the entire Amphibious Ready Group to support the Army's Operation Hastings.

The area of operations for Deckhouse III was the Vung Tau Peninsula, 60 miles (96 km) southeast of Saigon. The landings were carried out by U.S. Marines, paratroopers, and Australian units. The target area was the coastal areas of Binh Tuy and Phuoc provinces. This was an uncultivated plain containing jungle and swamps. The rifle companies operated over widely separated areas, relying on small-unit patrolling to search the area.

The U.S. Marines conducted Deckhouse IV, an amphibious search-and-destroy operation in conjunction with the ongoing Prairie I Operation, 8 miles (12.8 km) northeast of Dong Ha between August and September.

OPERATION DECKHOUSE

Location   coast of South Vietnam

Date   June–September, 1966

Commanders and forces   Viet Cong; U.S.: 5th Marine Division, Special Landing Force, 173rd Airborne Brigade

Casualties   VC: 750 killed; U.S.: 100 killed

Key actions   The support of the aircraft of the U.S. Seventh Fleet was responsible for many enemy casualties.

Key effects   The results were disappointing for the Americans as the enemy, except during Deckhouse IV, refused to stand and fight.

Operation Hastings was a search-and-destroy mission conducted 55 miles (88 km) northwest of Hue to counter the growing threat of the North Vietnamese 324B Division's movement across the Demilitarized Zone (DMZ). U.S. Marine and South Vietnamese commanders met in Hue in order to plan the operation. In addition, the Battalion Landing Team, 3rd Battalion, 5th Marine Regiment, would conduct Operation Deckhouse II to support Hastings.

The Marines go in

Placed under the command of Brigadier General Lowell E. English, USMC, the Marines launched a heliborne attack in order to secure landing sites in the enemy's rear areas. The heliborne lift at first enjoyed a relatively uneventful landing, but came under heavy fire as subsequent lifts touched down. Through the heavy use

American A-4 Skyhawk attack aircraft are prepared for a mission against the Viet Cong in mid-1966.

OPERATION HASTINGS

Location   Demilitarized Zone

Date   July 7–August 3, 1966

Commanders and forces   NVA: 324B Division; U.S.: 1st Marine Division; ARVN: 1st Division

Casualties   NVA: 882 dead; Free World: 51 killed, 162 wounded

Key actions   U.S. forces, together with their South Vietnamese allies, held the initiative throughout the entire offensive, forcing the North Vietnamese 324B Division across the border area along the DMZ back into North Vietnam.

Key effects   The Americans concluded that Operation Hastings had prevented a major North Vietnamese attack.

of intelligence-gathering reconnaissance teams from the Marines and ARVN, the Allied commanders were able to position their forces in areas where they could achieve good results. Many enemy positions were overrun and large quantities of equipment, clothing, and other supplies were captured by the Marines and ARVN troops. The North Vietnamese Army (NVA) soldiers at first chose to stand and fight, but soon tried to avoid contact with the Marines and ARVN. The Marines uncovered several recently abandoned enemy camp areas, with everything except weapons left in place. Included in this find was a regimental-sized command post large enough to hold 500 NVA troops in the Dong Ha Mountains.

Operation Hastings involved 8,000 U.S. Marines, 3,000 South Vietnamese, and perhaps as many as 12,500 enemy troops.

American troops burn an abandoned enemy jungle base during Operation Hastings in July 1966.

The 1st Cavalry Division (Airmobile) conducted a 513-day operation called Operation Byrd in Binh Thuan Province. At any given time, one to two battalions carried out simultaneous operations.

In order to protect the vital port of Phan Thiet and surrounding areas, the 1st Cavalry Division was ordered to defeat enemy forces in the Byrd area, in close cooperation with South Vietnamese forces. The U.S. troops were to assist in opening National Highway 1 as it ran along the coast through this area. On each day during the operation there were 1,600 troops in the field. Although the composition of the troops varied, the nucleus was airmobile troops in helicopters. The small force contained all the elements essential to sustain independent operations and could take advantage of all available support.

Heavy fire support

At first the Americans established a fire base and command post on the Phan Thiet airfield. From there troops were airlifted into landing zones within range of the support of the artillery battery. The first operations relieved pressure on Phan Thiet and the nearby towns. The U.S. troops then began combined operations with the South Vietnamese, taking advantage of U.S. Navy ships and U.S. Air Force fighters for fire support. The area of influence of the task force was then broadened by the establishment of more fire bases further from Phan Thiet.

OPERATION BYRD

Location Binh Thuan Province

Date August 26, 1966–January 20, 1968

Commanders and forces VC: two battalions; U.S.: 1st Cavalry Division (Airmobile); ARVN: 23d Division

Casualties VC: 849 killed; U.S.: 34 killed

Key actions Almost daily contacts with squad and platoon-size Viet Cong elements as the task force searched base areas and cut enemy lines of communication.

Key effects During the 17 months of Operation Byrd, the 2d Battalion, 7th Cavalry Regiment, had only 34 troopers killed in action while 849 enemy were killed and 109 captured. More important than enemy losses, the Americans had enabled the South Vietnamese government to spread its control from the province and district capitals to virtually all the population in the area.

OPERATION ATTLEBORO

ARVN troops on board an armored personal carrier attack a Viet Cong stronghold during Operation Attleboro.

Operation Attleboro was started by the 196th Light Infantry Brigade and was fought in two phases. Phase I started on September 2, 1966, and Phase II started about November 6, lasting to November 24. The purpose of the operation was to deny the Viet Cong (VC) strategic positions 50 miles (80 km) north of Saigon. Some of the operation took place inside the infamous "Iron Triangle," a communist sanctuary inside South Vietnam.

There was no significant contact with the enemy until October 19, when a sizeable enemy base area was uncovered. A major action took place on November 3 involving the U.S. 1st and 25th Infantry Divisions, 196th Light Infantry Brigade, 173rd Airborne Brigade, and two South Vietnamese battalions.

At its end, there were 1,106 confirmed enemy casualties. This figure was the largest number of enemy casualties recorded to date in the war.

OPERATION ATTLEBORO

Location   Tay Ninh Province, South Vietnam

Date   September 2–November 24, 1966

Commanders and forces   VC: 9th Division; Free World: U.S. 1st Infantry Division, U.S. 4th Infantry Division, U.S. 25th Infantry Division; ARVN: III Corps Mike Force

Casualties   VC: 1,106 killed; U.S.: 155 killed

Key actions   U.S. fighter aircraft flew 1,571 sorties, while B-52 Arc Light sorties numbered 26.

Key effects   While the 9th VC Division was knocked out for several months, the ultimate futility of the war became apparent when it was discovered that the division merely retreated to Cambodia, where it was rebuilt with men and equipment.

OPERATION THAYER I AND

Thayer I was one of the largest air assaults launched by the U.S. 1st Cavalry Division in the Vietnam War. Its mission was to rid Binh Dinh Province of North Vietnamese Army (NVA) and Viet Cong (VC) soldiers and the VC's political infrastructure. On September 16, troopers of the 1st Brigade discovered an enemy regimental hospital, a factory for making grenades, antipersonnel mines, and a variety of weapons. On September 19, U.S. soldiers traded fire with two NVA combat support companies.

Battle at Hoa Hoi

In the opening phase of Operation Thayer, enemy elements of the 7th and 8th battalions, 18th NVA Regiment, had been reported in the village of Hoa Hoi. The 1st battalion, 12th Cavalry Regiment, in the face of heavy resistance, deployed to encircle the village and trap the NVA soldiers. On October 2, B Company was the first to be air assaulted into the landing area east of the village. The Americans came under intense small-arms and mortar fire. A Company landed to the southwest and began a movement northeast to the village. In the meantime, C Company landed north of the village and began moving south. By this time A and B Companies had linked up and established positions which prevented the enemy from slipping out of the village during the night. The communists were trapped.

OPERATION THAYER I AND II

Location   Binh Dinh Province, South Vietnam

Date   September 1966 to February 1967

Commanders and forces   NVA: 610th Division, Viet Cong: 2d Regiment; U.S.: 1st Cavalry Division (Airmobile)

Casualties   NVA: 1,800 killed; U.S.: 204 killed

Key actions   On November 1, troopers of the 7th Cavalry Regiment became engaged in a sharp fight with the NVA 93rd Battalion and the 2d Viet Cong Regiment. The action took place in the vicinity of National Route 1 and Dam Tra-O Lake south of the Gay Giep mountains. It was a U.S. victory.

Key effects   The cohesion of VC and NVA organization in eastern Binh Dinh Province had been destroyed. The enemy was attempting to find shelter in the mountains and valleys surrounding the coastal plains and among the many villages and hamlets scattered through the rice-growing region. The Viet Cong administrative structure in the region was disrupted and VC tax-gathering, recruitment, and political operations were badly disorganized.

During the course of the evening, A and C Companies, 1st Battalion, 5th Cavalry Regiment, were airlifted into an area east of the village to assist in the destruction of the enemy. Additional support was called up in the form of howitzers of the 19th Artillery Regiment. These big guns helped to blast the enemy in the village.

Thayer comes to an end

In the morning of October 3, C Company, 1st Battalion, 12th Cavalry Regiment, and C Company, 1st Battalion, 5th Cavalry Regiment, attacked south to drive the remaining enemy forces into A and B Companies, who were dug in to strong blocking positions to take the attack. This last action broke the strong resistance of the enemy and the mission was completed.

On October 25, Operation Thayer II continued the drive to pacify Binh Dinh Province with success. The 1st Cavalry Division's Operation Thayer II wound down and ended in early February 1967.

The final verdict

This is what the U.S. Army had to say about the outcome of the campaign in Binh Dinh Province: "During October of 1966, allied military forces combined efforts in three closely co-ordinated operations to destroy the enemy in the central and eastern portions of the Republic of Vietnam's Binh Dinh Province and to uproot the Viet Cong's political structure along the province's populated coastal region. In a period of 22 days, the 22d ARVN Division, the Republic of Korea Capital Division, and the U.S. 1st Cavalry Division (Airmobile) were to dominate the battlefield to such an extent that the aggressor had only one alternative to fighting: surrender. The enemy not only suffered heavy personnel losses in decisive combat, but many of his vital logistic and support bases were discovered and destroyed. The victory meant that the central coastal portion of Binh Dinh Province and hundreds of thousands of citizens were returned to the control of the South Vietnamese government. The people of the province were freed from Viet Cong terrorism and extortion for the first time in many years."

OPERATION FAIRFAX

This operation, started by three battalions, one each from the U.S. 1st, 4th, and 25th Infantry Divisions, was conducted in the area immediately surrounding Saigon. The operation was designed to restore security around Saigon, where the Viet Cong (VC) was active. It emphasized joint U.S. and ARVN cooperation (American units worked in cooperation with ARVN troops). The U.S. operation terminated on December 14, 1967, when responsibility for security in the Fairfax operational area passed to the ARVN's 5th Ranger Group.

However, Fairfax was largely a failure. This led the Americans to rethink their strategy concerning defeating the VC. And in 1967 they introduced the Phoenix Program. This was a plan to to conduct arrest and assassination operations against suspected VC and VC sympathizers.

OPERATION FAIRFAX

Location   Saigon Capital Military District and Gia Dinh Province

Date   November 30, 1966–December 14, 1967

Commanders and forces   Viet Cong; U.S.: 1st, 4th, 25th Infantry Divisions, 196th Infantry Brigade

Casualties   VC: 1,043 killed; U.S.: 120 killed

Key actions   The cooperation between U.S. and ARVN units in Gia Binh Province was designed to put heart into South Vietnamese units.

Key effects   Security improved in Gia Binh by the end of 1967, but the VC were still able to collect taxes and recruit.

An American soldier uses a flamethrower to destroy an enemy shelter during Fairfax. Burning people's homes did nothing to improve relations between soldiers and civilians in South Vietnam.

As **1967 arrived,** U.S., South Vietnamese, and Allied forces in Vietnam were locked in a war becoming increasingly intense. More and more North Vietnamese Army (NVA) forces entered the conflict. As they penetrated into South Vietnam, U.S. forces upped the pace of military operations against both them and the Viet Cong (VC). The U.S. and South Vietnamese military undertook continuous offensives in and along the Demilitarized Zone (DMZ). Marines in I Corps Tactical Zone initiated offensives to cut off NVA forces' infiltration into the Northern and Central Highlands. The leathernecks also began setting up the "McNamara Line," a series of electronic sensors and warning systems, to warn the Allies of enemy movement in border areas. However, despite these measures Hanoi continued to send men and supplies down the Ho Chi Minh Trail. In the South Viet Cong activity increased as "Charlie" waged a bitter war against Saigon and its U.S. backer.

The Central Highlands

In the Central Highlands, the U.S. Army went over to the offensive and inflicted a series of punishing defeats on the enemy. In the area north of Saigon, the capital city of South Vietnam, U.S. Army infantry units—such as the 1st and 25th Infantry Divisions, as well as elements of the 7th and 101st Air Cavalry along with their Army of the Republic of Vietnam (ARVN) allies—launched several major offensives designed to clear out the infamous "Iron Triangle" that had served as a major base of operations for the North Vietnamese and VC.

The Mekong Delta

The U.S. Navy, meanwhile, kept up the pressure on the North Vietnamese and Viet Cong through its interception campaign in the Mekong Delta and inland waterways south of Saigon. U.S. Navy aircraft carriers served as floating platforms for launching repeated

Huey helicopters over South Vietnam. The one on the left has the Ace of Spades painted on its nose. This was regarded as a deadly omen by Viet Cong troops, and U.S. soldiers often left the Ace of Spades as a calling card to spread fear among the enemy.

sorties against North Vietnamese forces in support of U.S. ground operations in and around South Vietnam's long coastline. U.S. naval vessels likewise provided naval gunfire support for U.S., South Vietnamese, and Allied (South Korean and Australian) forces operating in unison with U.S. Marines and U.S. Army in the northern military districts and along South Vietnam's long coastline.

Air strikes against the North

The U.S. Air Force also maintained steady pressure on the enemy through its three-pronged offensive in the skies over South Vietnam and Laos, and bombing missions against the Ho Chi Minh Trail and Petroleum, Oil and Lubricants (POL) plants in North Vietnam. It also attacked the bridges and major rail networks which were ferrying supplies to points along the major supply routes heading straight toward South Vietnam.

Increasing American troop levels

On the political front, President Lyndon B. Johnson and his advisors struggled to maintain the pressure on North Vietnam, while seeking a political solution to end the war. The Johnson administration also sought to placate the so-called "doves" and the antiwar movement at home, which threatened not only to derail the American military campaign against North Vietnam but also to upset the "peace feelers" which the administration had sent out to North Vietnamese leaders. By so doing, Johnson hoped not only to discourage Hanoi's continued infiltration southward, but also to end its support to the National Liberation Front (Viet Cong). But his attempts failed.

As the war expanded—over 400,000 U.S. troops would be in Vietnam by 1967—so did the antiwar movement. For example, in April 1967 more than 300,000 people demonstrated against the war in New York. Six months later, 50,000 surrounded the Pentagon. In the United States support for the war was falling: by the fall of 1967, only 35 percent of Americans supported the war in Vietnam.

Operation Sam Houston started on January 1, 1967, but did not really get going until U.S. troops crossed the Nam Sathay River in mid-February. The purpose of the operation was to stop the movement of North Vietnamese troops and equipment into South Vietnam from communist bases inside Cambodia and Laos. In the next five weeks the Americans had nine major contacts and a number of small contacts with North Vietnamese Army (NVA) forces. It is significant to note that in each major contact, enemy tactics followed the same pattern. The communists located U.S. fire bases and kept them under constant surveillance. When the U.S. companies moved out on patrol, the enemy would keep track of their movements through the use of small reconnaissance parties or trail watchers. The favorite communist tactic involved a procedure of reporting movements back and, at a time and location of his choosing, attempting to destroy a rifle company while it was moving. The NVA would close quickly with the elements of the company before supporting artillery fire could be effectively employed.

Cedar Falls was designed to destroy the Viet Cong's headquarters, as well as preventing the movement of enemy forces into the major war zones in III Corps Tactical Zone and defeating Viet Cong units which were located there.

Like Operation Attleboro preceding it, Cedar Falls tapped the manpower and resources of nearly every U.S. Army unit in the corps area. A series of preliminary maneuvers brought army units into position, while several air assaults sealed off the area known as the Iron Triangle, making use of the natural barriers of the rivers that formed two of its boundaries.

OPERATION SAM HOUSTON

Location Pleiku and Kontum Provinces, South Vietnam

Date January 1–April 5, 1967

Commanders and forces NVA: 1st Division; U.S.: 4th and 25th Infantry Divisions

Casualties NVA: 733 killed; U.S.: 169 killed

Key actions NVA units attempted to surround entire companies and fragment them into smaller platoon-sized pieces using mortars and large numbers of snipers in the trees. NVA mortars were countered with U.S. artillery and air attacks, plus small-arms fire.

Key effects Degraded the NVA's 1st Division's attempt to operate from bases inside Cambodia.

Soldiers of the 1st Infantry Division rapel from a CH-47 Chinook helicopter to clear a landing zone for helicopters during Operation Cedar Falls, January 8, 1967.

Then American units began a series of sweeps to push the enemy toward the blocking forces. As Cedar Falls progressed throughout January and into February, U.S. troops destroyed hundreds of enemy fortifications, captured large quantities of supplies and food, and evacuated the hamlets. But contact with the enemy was fleeting. Most of the Viet Cong, including the high-level cadre of the regional command, had escaped by infiltrating through Allied lines.

OPERATION CEDAR FALLS

Location Iron Triangle, South Vietnam

Date January 8–26, 1967

Commanders and forces VC: 1st, 7th, and 8th Viet Cong Main Force Battalions of Military Region IV; U.S.: 1st, 25th Infantry Divisions, 173rd Airborne Brigade, 11th Armored Cavalry Brigade

Casualties VC: 720 dead; U.S. 72 dead; ARVN: 11 dead

Key actions At the village of Ben Suc, on January 5–8, long under the control of the Viet Cong, 60 helicopters descended into seven landing zones in less than a minute. Ben Suc was surrounded and its entire population evacuated, before the village and tunnel complex were destroyed. But the Viet Cong had fled before the helicopters arrived.

Key effects Cedar Falls demonstrated the value of extended operations within VC-controlled areas. The length of the operation gave the small unit commanders and the troops enough time to become familiar with the terrain as well as the VC situation. Unlike many other operations where troops went into an area for two or three day search-and-destroy missions, Cedar Falls provided the much-needed long-term effort to effectively accomplish the mission. VC equipment losses were 23 crew-served weapons, 590 individual weapons, and over 2,800 explosive items such as mines, grenades, and mortar and artillery rounds.

OPERATION PERSHING

Private James Hembree of the 1st Air Cavalry Division cools himself off during Operation Pershing.

The 1st Air Cavalry Division commenced Operation Pershing where it had conducted Operation Thayer during the previous year. The operation was designed to eliminate the communist enemy from this rice-rich coastal province.

Under the command of Major General John Tolson, the division conducted search-and-destroy operations with ARVN forces to destroy the Viet Cong infrastructure and help establish South Vietnamese control. Tolson carried out more than 900 such operations using the division's 450 helicopters. When communist forces retreated from remote areas, 1st Cavalry units removed the inhabitants. Air force aircraft then sprayed the depopulated areas with Agent Orange to deny the VC hiding areas.

Until September the entire division operated throughout Binh Dinh, but by December Pershing had become a holding operation, with only one brigade remaining in the province.

OPERATION PERSHING

Location Binh Dinh Province, South Vietnam

Date February 11, 1967–January 19, 1968

Commanders and forces NVA: 3d Division, 22d Division; U.S.: 1st Cavalry Division (Airmobile); ARVN: 22d Regiment

Casualties VC/NVA: 5,401 killed; U.S.: 600 killed

Key actions From December 6 to 20, the 1st Brigade and the 1st Battalion, 50th Infantry (Mechanized), and the 22d ARVN Regiment killed 650 NVA near Tam Quan in the last major battle of Pershing.

Key effects The Bong Son Plain was cleared of NVA and VC forces.

This was the largest operation of the Vietnam war to date. Like the Iron Triangle, War Zone C was a major Viet Cong stronghold and had been a sanctuary for insurgents for over 20 years. It was also believed to be the location of headquarters of the enemy's Central Office of South Vietnam (COSVN). However, owing to the remoteness of the area and the strict secrecy with which the enemy treated the headquarters, few facts were known about it and units in the area.

The operation was conducted in two major phases. Junction City I placed blocking forces near the Cambodian border in a horseshoe configuration. The 1st Infantry Division forces occupied the northern and eastern portions, as a search and destroy force drove north. Phase II included two major battles.

An American B-52 Stratofortress bomber is loaded with weapons before setting off to bomb communist bases in Tay Ninh Province.

OPERATION JUNCTION CITY

Location War Zone C, northern Tay Ninh Province, South Vietnam

Date February 22–May 14, 1967

Commanders and forces VC: 9th Division; U.S.: 1st, 4th, and 25th Infantry Divisions, 196th Infantry Brigade, 11th Armored Cavalry Regiment and 173rd Airborne Brigade; ARVN: Cavalry Troop and 36th Ranger Battalion

Casualties VC/NVA: 2,728 killed; U.S.: 282 killed

Key actions There were three major battles, each intiated by the Viet Cong: the first at Ap Bau Bang; the second at Fire Support Base Gold, and the third at Ap Gu. In each battle, the Viet Cong attacked U.S. forces and were repulsed, suffering very heavy losses.

Key effects The Viet Cong headquarters, one of the targets of the operation, was not captured and, once the U.S. troops withdrew, the area was reoccupied by the communists.

The Khe Sanh combat base, originally established by the Green Berets in August 1962, was located in the Quang Tri Province in the northwest corner of South Vietnam, close to the North Vietnamese supply route to the south known as the Ho Chi Minh Trail. The base sat atop a plateau in the shadow of Dong Tri Mountain and overlooked a tributary of the Quang Tri River. It was a useful observation post, serving as a platform for launching special operations missions and road-watch teams which monitored North Vietnamese Army (NVA) activities in Laos. The Khe Sanh airstrip was improved in the spring of 1967. The base had artillery support, and its area of operations was within the range of the 175mm guns of Camp Carroll, to the east.

The stronghold of Khe Sanh

Khe Sanh had become the westernmost obstacle in the series of obstacles in I Corps Tactical Zone. General Westmoreland knew that Khe Sanh was not only a defensive perimeter, and a screen for NVA and communist infiltration. It was also a place where the enemy could be hit with close air support, artillery fire, and machine-gun fire.

On April 24, a major battle broke out. This signaled the commencement of heavy fighting between the U.S. Marines and the NVA throughout the summer of 1967. The 3rd Marines arrived at Khe Sanh on April 25 and 26, 1967. On April 27, a second artillery battery was

The base and airstrip at Khe Sanh, as seen from a U.S. aircraft. The airstrip was the only way to get into and out of the base.

dispatched there as well. Immediately upon arrival, the Marines moved out to establish a perimeter on the outlying hills of the air base. On May 3, 1967, in some of the heaviest fighting of the Vietnam War to date, the U.S. Marines seized Hill 881N, northwest of the base. This position afforded a position overlooking the enemy's infiltration routes. The 3rd Marines had rid the three hills (861, 881N, 8881S) of all NVA forces by May 11. However, throughout the rest of 1967 the NVA would continue to build up its strength around the base, ready for another attack.

BATTLE OF KHE SANH

Location   Khe Sanh, South Vietnam

Date   April 24 –May 11, 1967

Commanders and forces   NVA; U.S.: 3rd Marine Regiment

Casualties   NVA; 940 killed; U.S.: 155 killed

Key actions   On May 11, the First Battle of Khe Sanh ended as the Marines defending the fire base beat off a furious NVA attack.

Key effects   Firepower again proved decisive. During the fighting, the 1st Marine Aircraft Wing flew more than 1,110 sorties and dropped 1,900 tons (1,930 tonnes) of bombs on a series of NVA concrete-reinforced fortifications on top of Hill 881. While Marine aircraft provided ground infantry with close air support during the operation, the U.S. Air Force carried out 23 B-52 strikes—known as "arc light" strikes—against enemy troop concentrations, supply and ammunition depots, and communications. U.S. Marine and army artillery units fired more than 25,000 rounds at the enemy in support of the Marines around Khe Sanh.

The U.S. Marine mission during Hickory was to remove enemy forces and installations from the southern half of the Demilitarized Zone (DMZ). This was the first time the Marines had ventured into the DMZ in force. Their attack was supported by a massive U.S. Navy, Marine, and Air Force effort, and a parallel sweep by the 1st ARVN Division.

On May 18, the Marines attacked and became involved in heavy fighting that lasted 48 hours and killed 61 enemy. Before daybreak, five battalions of the 1st ARVN Division moved north from Gio Linh along the axis of Route 1 to just below where Freedom Bridge crosses the Ben Hai, then peeled off the road to the right and left and began sweeping southward.

The assault followed a tight time schedule to take advantage of the preparatory bombardment being delivered by five destroyers and two cruisers offshore. Hickory was one of several Marine operations carried out in and around the DMZ, all of which were quite successful (see map below).

OPERATION HICKORY

Location   Quang Tri Province, South Vietnam

Date   May 18-28, 1967

Commanders and forces   NVA; U.S.: 1st Marine Division

Casualties   NVA: 815 Killed; U.S.: 119 killed

Key actions   On May 18, a huge 700-round 105mm and 155mm artillery salvo hammered NVA fortifications near the village of Phu An. Then fighter aircraft let loose 750 and 1000lb bombs and inundated the area with napalm.

Key effects   The NVA had been served notice that the southern half of the DMZ would no longer be a sanctuary. Their command and control arrangements had been disrupted, they had lost much in supplies and ammunition, and their fortifications had been dismantled.

Operation Lam Son-54 was initiated by two ARVN battalions from the 1st ARVN Division. On May 18, 1967, U.S. Marines moved north into the Demilitarized Zone (DMZ). Their mission was "to remove enemy forces and installations from the southern half of the DMZ." Under control of the 9th Marine Regiment, this was the first time the Marines had ventured into the DMZ in force. Their attack was supported by a massive Navy-Marine-Air Force effort, and a parallel sweep by the 1st ARVN Division in Lam Son-54. Before daybreak on May 16, five battalions of the 1st ARVN Division moved north from Gio Linh along the axis of Route 1 to just below where Freedom Bridge crosses the Ben Hai. They then peeled off the road to the right and left, and began sweeping southward. Making no contact, the South Vietnamese units proceeded to the Ben Hai River, located in the center of the DMZ itself, and started sweeping south.

While the two battalions were advancing on the east side of Highway 1, three ARVN airborne battalions did the same on the west. On May 19, the 31st and 812th NVA regiments met the ARVN multibattalion sweep and fierce fighting ensued that would continue for more than a week.

Overall results

The Allied operations in and around the DMZ resulted in half a dozen enemy battalions being caught off guard south of the DMZ. At least 815 of the enemy were dead: 445 killed by the Marines, 370 by the ARVN. The southern half of the DMZ was no longer a communist sanctuary.

A U.S. armored personnel carrier moves through the swamps of the Mekong Delta in search of the Viet Cong.

This was a Mobile Riverine Force (MRF) operation designed to destroy Cho Gao District Company and enhance the security of Cho Gao Canal in Dinh Tuong Province. The Mobile Riverine Force was a joint U.S. Navy–Army force created in mid-1966 for search-and-destroy operations in the Mekong Delta (this important rice-producing area covers about one-fourth of Vietnam but contains around half of the country's population). From June 1967 onward, Operation Coronado concentrated on Long An and Dinh Tuong Provinces in the Mekong Delta, with special attention to the Rung Sat Special Zone.

At the end of Operation Coronado on July 26, the Mobile Riverine Force had killed 478 of the enemy.

OPERATION LAM SON-54

Location Quang Tri Province, South Vietnam

Date May 16-28, 1967

Commanders and forces NVA: 31st and 812th Regiments; ARVN: 1st Division

Casualties NVA: 370 killed, 30 captured, and 51 assorted weapons seized; ARVN: 22 killed, 122 wounded

Key actions Most of the ARVN's casualties were caused by enemy mortars and rockets in the area dubbed by U.S. troops as the "rocket belt," north of Dong Ha.

Key effects The operation boosted ARVN morale.

OPERATION CORONADO

Location Dinh Tuong Province, South Vietnam

Date June 1-July 26, 1967

Commanders and forces Viet Cong; US: 2d Brigade. 9th Infantry Division, Mobile Riverine Force

Casualties VC: 478 killed; U.S.: 40 killed

Key actions The MRF searched out the Viet Cong's main force and local battalions in a combination of riverine, search-and-destroy, patrolling, and interdiction operations.

Key effects Initially, the VC attempted to stand and fight against the MRF hammer and anvil tactics, but the sheer scale of the MRF operations swept the VC aside.

DA NANG

Da Nang Air Base was an important Republic of Vietnam Air Force (VNAF) facility.

During the night of July 14/15, North Vietnamese Army (NVA) and Viet Cong (VC) rocket units moved out of "Happy Valley," southwest of Da Nang, and set up six firing positions, which were divided into two clusters of three positions each. Each firing position contained six individual launcher sites. Shortly after midnight (July 14), the enemy rocket sites opened fire on the airfield of Da Nang. Within five minutes 50 projectiles hit the base. U.S. Marines were quick to react after the launching of the first volley of rockets. A circling U.S. Air Force fighter-bomber spotted the first launching sites and opened fire. But during the attack the Marines lost 10 aircraft, 13 barracks, and a bomb dump, with 41 VNAF aircraft destroyed.

DA NANG

Location Quang Nam Province, South Vietnam

Date July 14-15, 1967

Commanders and forces NVA & VC; U.S. Marines

Casualties unknown

Key actions On July 15, an early morning enemy rocket attack on aircraft at the southern end of the Da Nang Air Base resulted in heavy damage. The NVA and Viet Cong fired 50 rounds of 122mm rockets at the air base, the first use of these Soviet-supplied long-range weapons. Ten jets were destroyed and 41 damaged..

Key effects After this encounter, not only had the communists succeeded in destroying a large quantity of material, but they had also scored a major propaganda coup, as the attack illustrated to the 300,000 South Vietnamese who inhabited the area that the communists could strike wherever they wanted. The attack also forced the Marines to make readjustments to the defense of the airfield. To counter the NVA's claim that it could strike whenever and wherever it wanted, the U.S. 1st Marine Division launched a psychological operation (PsyOps) campaign, which later proved to be effective in countering this enemy threat.

Wrecked aircraft litter the tarmac at Da Nang following the communist rocket attacks in July 1967.

OPERATION KINGFISHER

This was an operation conducted in the Demilitarized Zone (DMZ) by the U.S. 3d Marine Division. Its aim was to prevent North Vietnamese Army (NVA) incursions into Quang Tri Province. The Marines were ordered to find, fix, fight, and finish any NVA found in the DMZ south of the Ben Hai River. Beginning on July 16, there was minimal contact with the NVA until July 28, when the 2d Battalion, 9th Marine Regiment, supported by tanks, went into the DMZ along Route 606. It came under heavy artillery fire from prepared enemy positions along Route 606. The battalion suffered heavy casualties and had to be supported by U.S. air strikes.

Battle at Con Thien

On September 10, the 3d Battalion, 26th Marine Regiment, fought the NVA 812th Regiment at Con Thien and suffered over 200 casualties. Eleven days later, the 2d Battalion, 4th Marine Regiment, was engaged in bitter fighting with the NVA's 90th Regiment at Con Thien. Before the end of September the NVA launched three more attacks against Con Thien, firing more than 3,000 mortar and rocket rounds. But the base held. The Americans retaliated by massing one of the greatest concentrations of firepower in support of a single division during the entire Vietnam War. However, by early October the 2d Battalion, 4th Marine Regiment, had been reduced from 952 to 462 men. The last major operation of Kingfisher took place between October 25 and 28. The operation had been a bruising encounter for the Marines, and they had taken heavy losses. But they had inflicted greater losses on the enemy.

OPERATION KINGFISHER

Location Demilitarized Zone, South Vietnam

Date July 16–October 31, 1967

Commanders and forces NVA: 90th & 812th Regiments; U.S.: 3d Marine Division

Casualties NVA: 1,117 killed; U.S.: 340 dead, 1,461 wounded

Key actions In a minor incident, Marines uncovered an NVA base along Route 9. This discovery led to the halting of vehicle convoys into the nearby Khe Sanh base, which from July onward had to be supplied by air.

Key effects The Marines beat off some of the best units in the NVA.

AIR STRIKES AGAINST THE NORTH

As part of the The Rolling Thunder campaign, U.S. B-52 bombers struck targets in southern North Vietnam. Rolling Thuunder had a three-fold purpose: to raise the morale of the South Vietnamese, impose a penalty on Hanoi for supporting aggression in the South, and reduce infiltration of men and supplies into the South. The air campaign was also based on the hope that the gradual destruction of North Vietnam's military bases and constant attacks on its lines of communications would bring its leaders to the negotiating table. President Johnson retained such firm control of the air campaign against the North that no important target or new target areas could be hit without his approval. His decisions were relayed through Secretary McNamara to the Joint Chiefs, who then issued strike directives to commanders in the Pacific. The latter then earmarked targets among the U.S. Air Force (USAF), U.S. Navy, and the Vietnamese Air Force (VNAF), with USAF crews normally providing air cover for the VNAF. The VNAF later withdrew from northern operations to concentrate on supporting ARVN forces within South Vietnam.

A revised Rolling Thunder target list, issued on July 20, 1967, permitted air attacks on 16 additional fixed

A USAF F-100 attack aircraft of the 352d Tactical Fighter Squadron releases a bomb over North Vietnam in August 1967.

targets and 23 road, rail, and waterway segments inside the restricted Hanoi–Haiphong area. Between August 13 and 19, bridges, bypasses, railyards, and military storage areas were bombed in an effort to slow or halt traffic between the two cities and to points north and south. On August 2, Hanoi's famous Paul Doumer rail and highway bridge was hit for the first time. The center span was knocked down and two other spans were damaged. Struck again on October 25, another span went down and finally, on December 19, the rebuilt center span was dropped again.

AIR STRIKES AGAINST THE NORTH

Location North Vietnam

Date August 13-19, 1967

Commanders and forces NVA; U.S.: President Johnson

Casualties unknown

Key actions Raids were designed to sever communications between Hanoi and Haiphong, the most important deep water port in the North.

Key effects Some 30 percent of the North's railroad system was destroyed.

ARC LIGHT STRIKES

A B-52 is loaded with bombs just before an Arc Light bombing mission against the North Vietnamese Army.

The first B-52 Arc Light bombing mission was carried out on June 18, 1965. On this mission, 27 B-52F bombers of the 7th and 320th Bombardment Wings based at Guam in the Pacific Ocean were used to attack a Viet Cong jungle redoubt. During that year, the B-52s flew approximately 9,700 effective bombing sorties, almost twice the number flown in 1966.

On September 1, 1967, B-52 bombers conducted a series of "arc light" strikes against NVA troop and artillery positions north of the DMZ. U.S. Army and Marine artillery also pounded NVA positions north of the DMZ and, ultimately, managed to relieve the pressure on Con Thien.

ARC LIGHT STRIKES

Location North Vietnam

Date September 1, 1967

Commanders and forces US: Strategic Air Command (General Joseph J. Nazzaro)

Casualties unknown

Key actions The deployment of B-52s to U Tapao Royal Thai Air Base on April 10, 1967, meant a much shorter trip to the target area and back, and no need for tanker support except for backup. Initially, U Tapao was used as a forward base. Bombers would perform a raid from Anderson on Guam to land at U Tapao, conduct eight more raids out of Thailand, and then perform a final raid that would end back at Anderson. At that time, U Tapao lacked the facilities for really extensive service on the B-52s, and so any serious work had to be performed back at Anderson.

Key effects The B-52 bomber was instrumental in deterring NVA incursions into the DMZ.

Whoever held the fire base at Con Thien, "Hill of Angels," 2 miles (3.2 km) south of the Demilitarized Zone (DMZ), had an unobstructed view for a dozen miles in every direction. It had been under pressure since the spring of 1967, but it was not until September 1967 that the North Vietnamese Army (NVA) started its major assault. Every day 152mm howitzers, 120mm and 82mm mortars, and 122mm rockets shelled the Marines that guarded Con Thien. During the climax of the attack (September 19–27, 1967) over 3,000 rounds of artillery pounded the base, almost wiping it off the map. On September 25, a reported 1,200 rounds pounded the base.

NVA deception

Some enemy bunkers were very close to Con Thien. Eliminating them could be a matter of life or death. One Marine recounted meeting enemy soldiers dressed as U.S. Marines. The platoon sergeant told his men not to fire, until he looked through his fieldglasses and saw that they were NVA with black sneakers on. The North Vietnamese had already killed several Marines before the sergeant called in an air strike and napalm that devastated the surrounding trees and the enemy base.

The Marine Corps rotated troops in and out of Con Thien every 30 days. Several other battalions would destroy bunker complexes. On many occasions the Marines would be ambushed and then pinned down with mortars. An average of 500 artillery rounds were fired daily into the small hilltop. But the Marines held; they also beat off several mass ground assaults.

CON THIEN

Location	Que Son Basin, South Vietnam
Date	September 19–27, 1967
Commanders and forces	NVA: General Giap; U.S.: 9th Marine Regiment, one battery of 105mm artillery, a platoon of tanks from Alpha Company, 3rd Tanks, an Ontos platoon, 4.2in mortars
Casualties	NVA: 376 killed; U.S.: 114 killed
Key actions	On September 25, 1,200 shells roared into the tiny area.
Key effects	The constant threat of North Vietnamese Army attacks increased the paranoia in the camp, while the emotional stress was wearing away at Marine morale. It was also cold at Con Thien during the monsoon season.

Viet Cong units assaulted Loc Ninh, site of the South Vietnamese Civilian Irregular Defense Group (CIDG) unit and the district command post. Loc Ninh was a village situated 80 miles (128 km) north of Saigon near the Cambodian border. As such, it was a focal point for Viet Cong (VC) incursions into South Vietnam. The location of the CIDG camp at Loc Ninh was a threat to the VC's easy passage. The communists therefore decided to destroy the camp.

U.S. helicopters ferry troops and supplies to the Cambodian border area in late 1967 to stop a Viet Cong invasion.

On October 9, 1967, the VC launched their assault. Supported by mortars and machine-gun fire, the VC fighters breached the defensive perimeter, but intense air and artillery fire prevented the complete loss of the post. Within a few hours, South Vietnamese and U.S. reinforcements reached Loc Ninh. Their arrival was enabled by the failure of the communists to seize the local airstrip. When the buildup ended, 10 U.S. Army battalions were positioned within Loc Ninh between the town and the Cambodian border. During the next days, Allied units fought off repeated enemy attacks ommunist forces tried desperately to score a victory. tical air support and artillery fire prevented the enemy e from penetrating the outnumbered U.S. and South namese Army positions. A total of 452 close air port and eight B-52 Arc Light bomber strikes, as well as estimated 30,152 rounds of artillery, had been directed inst the enemy. Once again American firepower had ed an isolated outpost.

On December 4, 1967, the Mobile Riverine Base moved to Sa Dec in the Mekong Delta. Its troops began operations to find and destroy Viet Cong (VC) elements in western Dinh Tuong and eastern Kien Phong Provinces. The battle that ensued on December 4–5 proved to be one of the most severe the Mobile Riverine Force had yet experienced.

Early on December 4, the VC attacked the boats with rockets and automatic weapons and a decision was made to land U.S. troops to the north of the enemy position. Shortly afterward more troops were landed south of the enemy position. Fighting was intense. In mid-afternoon, the troops made a frontal assault that overran the VC's major bunker complex. Supporting fire from armed helicopters and assault craft contributed largely to the success of the assault. The battle came to an end the next day.

A heavily armed Monitor of the Mobile Riverine Force leads a river assault flotilla in the Mekong Delta.

BATTLE OF LOC NINH

Location 80 miles (128 km) north of Saigon, South Vietnam

Date October 9–November 8, 1967

Commanders and forces VC: 272d and 273rd Regiments; U.S.: Civilian rregular Defense Group (CIDG), Special Forces, 1st Infantry Division

Casualties VC: 800 killed; U.S.: 15 killed

Key actions The final engagement occurred on November 7, when two ompanies of U.S. Infantry fought off the 3rd Battalion of the 272d Viet Cong Regiment.

Key effects Loc Ninh served as a "lightning rod" which attracted U.S. orces to the border and away from the cities and villages. Artillery, armed elicopters, and air strikes supported the U. S. troops. Although 15 U. S. roops died in heavy fighting, enemy losses were far higher. The battle of oc Ninh ended with the shattered remnants of the two VC regiments ithdrawing into the mountains.

OPERATIONS IN THE MEKONG DELTA

Location Dinh Tuong and eastern Kien Phong Provinces, South Vietnam

Date December 4–5, 1967

Commanders and forces VC: 267th Main Force, 502d Local Force Battalions; U.S.: Mobile Riverine Force

Casualties VC: 266 killed; ARVN: 40 killed, 107 wounded; U.S.: 9 killed, 89 wounded

Key actions The Mobile Riverine Force's attack on December 4 resulted in a U.S. victory.

Key effects The Viet Cong was for a while forced out of Dinh Tuong and eastern Kien Phong Provinces.

For the US military, the Tet Offensive was the turning point in the Vietnam War. Between 1965 and 1967, the war had increasingly been fought by American forces. The Army of the Republic of Vietnam (ARVN) trained and fought alongside the Americans, but it was obvious that more needed to be done to prepare it to take over control of the war. The North Vietnamese continued their preparations for a major offensive during the Tet holiday through January 1968, and the Viet Cong likewise prepared for assaults on South Vietnam's capital, Saigon, and other major cities in order to inflict psychological damage on the American military effort. The North Vietnamese still managed to maintain their monthly delivery of men and materiel down along the Ho Chi Minh Trail, in the process receiving more than their share of attention from the U.S. Air Force and Navy in bombing missions. These, however, failed to stop the flow of supplies.

Defense and counterattack

Even as the North Vietnamese Army (NVA) and Viet Cong (VC) prepared to launch a major offensive during the Tet celebration, General Westmoreland kept up the pressure on the enemy. Despite the siege at the US Marine Corps fire base at Khe Sanh and the Special Forces camp at Lang Vei, west of Khe Sanh, as well as at bases throughout the north of the country near the Demilitarized Zone (DMZ), U.S. soldiers continued to extract a huge price in manpower from the enemy as they forged ahead with General Westmoreland's war of attrition in the hopes that Hanoi and its two sponsors, the People's Republic of China and the Soviet Union, would fold under unrelenting U.S. pressure.

After blunting the Tet Offensive, U.S. forces went after the enemy in an all-out offensive which General Westmoreland hoped would put the enemy on the defensive once and for all. Politically, the Tet Offensive and the year 1968 in general would be one of disengagement for the United States as, before the entire nation, President Johnson placed a bombing halt on North Vietnam. The president also announced that

U.S. Marines at the base at Khe Sanh take shelter in a ditch during a North Vietnamese Army bombardment of the camp.

not only was he willing to discuss peace with North Vietnam's leaders but also that, much to his countrymen's surprise, he would not seek re-election in the fall elections of 1968.

Although the Tet Offensive broke the spirit of the Johnson Administration as it sought negotiations over the fighting, militarily the Tet Offensive and 1968 in general saw the North Vietnamese take savage punishment. The NVA failed to take Khe Sanh or Hue City during two prolonged and bloody battles with the U.S. Marines and ARVN forces. For the Viet Cong, Tet was even more severe. The bulk of its cadres died in major assaults against Saigon, Hue City, and several other major U.S.. military bases at Da Nang, Quang Tri, Bien Hoa, and Qui Nhon. But Hanoi saw the Tet Offensive and 1968 as the "beginning of the end" of its quest to unify the country.

The war in 1969

As 1969 was to demonstrate, there was still a lot of hard fighting to do in Vietnam. With it came the additional task of preparing the Army of the Republic of Vietnam to assume more and more of the fighting as U.S. forces began the slow but steady pace of redeployment. Yet even with the announced withdrawals of U.S. forces, the fighting on the ground in Vietnam continued, with the tempo of operations increasing. American troops faced an even more determined adversary on the battlefields, that stretched from the DMZ and Central Highlands to the marshes and rivers surrounding Saigon. U.S. military strength in South Vietnam peaked at 539,000 men and women, but the fighting became harder as both sides now positioned themselves for the peace negotiations, which got under way in Paris as a new U.S. president entered office. Determined to bring "peace with honor," President Nixon and his National Security Advisor, Henry Kissinger, reassured South Vietnamese President Nguyen Van Thieu that the United States would not "cut and run" in its commitment to defend South Vietnam against communist aggression. But privately both Americans sought disengagement from an unpopular war that continued to take hundreds of American lives.

The purpose of the Vietnamese Tet Offensive was to attack military and civilian command and control centers throughout South Vietnam, and to spark a general uprising among the population that would then topple the Saigon government. The operations are referred to as the Tet Offensive because they began during the early morning hours of January 30, 1968, the day of Tet. This important Vietnamese holiday celebrates the first day of the year on the traditional lunar calendar. Both North and South Vietnam had announced on national radio broadcasts that there would be a three-day ceasefire in honor of the Tet holiday.

The offensive begins

A wave of Viet Cong (VC) attacks began on the morning of January 30 in I and II Corps Tactical Zones (see map at right). When the main communist operation began the next morning, the offensive was countrywide and well coordinated, with more than 80,000 VC troops striking more than 100 towns and cities, including 36 of 44 provincial capitals, 5 of the 6 autonomous cities, 72 of 245 district towns, and the national capital, Saigon. The offensive was the largest military operation conducted by either side up to that point in the war.

The initial communist attacks stunned Allied forces and took them completely by surprise. In Saigon, for example, a 19-man VC squad attacked the

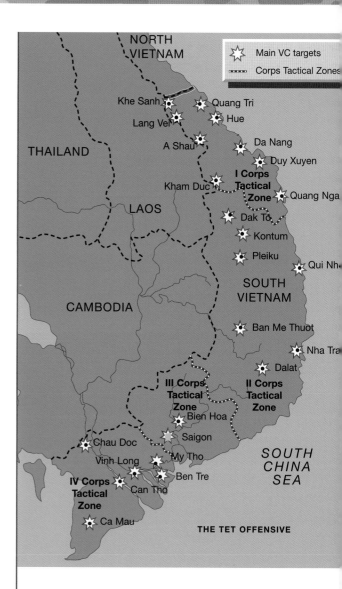

THE TET OFFENSIVE

Map legend:
- ☆ Main VC targets
- ▪▪▪ Corps Tactical Zones

Map labels: NORTH VIETNAM, Khe Sanh, Lang Vei, Quang Tri, Hue, THAILAND, A Shau, Da Nang, Duy Xuyen, Kham Duc, I Corps Tactical Zone, Quang Ngai, LAOS, Dak To, Kontum, Pleiku, Qui Nhon, SOUTH VIETNAM, CAMBODIA, Ban Me Thuot, Nha Trang, Dalat, III Corps Tactical Zone, II Corps Tactical Zone, Bien Hoa, Chau Doc, Saigon, SOUTH CHINA SEA, Vinh Long, My Tho, IV Corps Tactical Zone, Ben Tre, Can Tho, Ca Mau

---

TET OFFENSIVE

Location South Vietnam

Date January 30–September 23, 1968

Commanders and forces NVA/VC: General Giap, U.S. and Allied: General William C. Westmoreland

Casualties NVA/VC: 85,000 killed; South Vietnamese: 16,900 killed (military & civilian); U.S.: 3,400 killed

Key actions The failure of the communists to take the old imperial capital of Hue, where intense combat lasted for a month, and the U.S. combat base at Khe Sanh, where fighting continued for two more months, meant the offensive was bound to fail.

Key effects The Tet Offensive proved a turning point in the war. The American people were shocked that the VC/NVA possessed the strength to make the widespread strikes. The policy of Vietnamization (that South Vietnam should fight the war with its own forces) was launched, and many Americans concluded that the war was too costly to pursue.

U.S. Embassy. Although it never got into the building itself, the VC attack on the symbol of American power in Vietnam was broadcast around the world. This was a great propaganda victory for the communists, even though all the attackers were eventually killed by embassy guards. Throughout South Vietnam most of the communist attacks failed. They were quickly contained and beaten back by U.S. and ARVN forces, inflicting massive casualties on the attackers. However, in the United States news of the offensive contributed toward the general war weariness in the country and fueled antiwar protests. Many ordinary Americans now wanted the country to withdraw from the war.

SIEGE OF KHE SANH

The siege of the U.S. Marine base began on January 21, 1968, when the NVA began to shell it. An incessant barrage kept Khe Sanh's Marine defenders, which included three battalions from the 26th Marine Regiment, elements of the 9th Marine Regiment, and the South Vietnamese 37th Ranger Battalion, pinned down in their trenches and bunkers. Because the base had to be resupplied by air, the Americans were reluctant to put in any more troops and drafted a battle plan calling for massive artillery and air strikes.

During the siege, U.S. aircraft dropped 5,000 bombs daily. The relief of Khe Sanh, called Operation Pegasus, began in early April as the 1st Cavalry (Airmobile) Division and a South Vietnamese battalion approached from the east and south, while the Marines pushed westward to reopen Route 9. The siege was finally lifted on April 6.

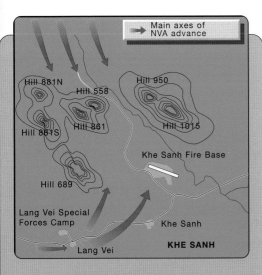

SIEGE OF KHE SANH

Location 14 miles (22.4 km) below the DMZ, South Vietnam

Date January 21–April 6, 1968

Commanders and forces NVA: 320th, 324th, 325C Divisions (Tran Quy Hai); U.S.: 26th Marine Regiment (Colonel David E. Lownds)

Casualties NVA: 10–15,000 killed; U.S.: 730 killed

Key actions On February 23, North Vietnamese artillery gunners and mortars fired more than 1,300 shells at Khe Sanh. This was the heaviest shelling of the base during the siege, but the Marines held.

Key effects As with the Tet Offensive in general, Khe Sanh damaged the trust and faith of the American people in their government, because the North's attack suggested that public officials appeared to have been lying about progress in the war and the strength of the communists.

BATTLE FOR HUE

The battle for Hue was the bloodiest action of the Tet Offensive. The cultural center of Vietnam, the city's Citadel and the Imperial Palace of Peace were two key communist targets. In January 1968, the headquarters of the ARVN 1st Division was located in the city, together with 200 U.S. troops and a few Australians. The battle began on January 31, when NVA units attacked the Citadel and the ARVN headquarters. The Palace of Peace was soon captured by the communists, but the Citadel held out.

Troops from the U.S. 1st Division at Phu Bar were despatched to relieve the city, but the communists were difficult to dislodge. On February 2, soldiers of the U.S. 1st Cavalry Division were landed to the northwest of the city. They ran into a strong communist blocking force. Meanwhile, the Marines continued to send troops into Hue. There followed two weeks of bitter street fighting. On February 25 the Imperial Palace was recaptured. The Battle for Hue was over.

BATTLE FOR HUE

Location Hue, South Vietnam

Date January 31–February 25, 1968

Commanders and forces NVA: 4th & 6th Regiments; ARVN: 1st Division; U.S.: 1st & 5th Marine Regiments, 1st Airborne Division

Casualties NVA: 5,000 killed; ARVN: 384 killed; U.S.: 649 killed

Key actions 50 percent of the city was destroyed, leaving 116,000 civilians homeless out of a population of 140,000.

Key effects The slaughter of 2,800 civilians by the NVA during the battle turned the population against the communist North.

This was an operation to relieve Khe Sanh. The plan involved the 1st Cavalry Division attacking west from Ca Lu to seize the high ground along Highway 9 in a series of air mobile assaults. At the same time U.S. Marines were to secure and repair the highway leading to Khe Sanh. On the first day of the operation, eight B-52 raids were flown to assist the ground forces as the 1st Cavalry Division attacked. By mid-April it was apparent that the enemy had chosen to flee rather than face the highly mobile Americans. Vast amounts of new equipment were abandoned in place by the North Vietnamese as they hastily retreated.

OPERATION PEGASUS

Location   Quang Tri Province

Date   April 1–15, 1968

Commanders and forces   NVA: 304th Division; U.S.: 1st Cavalry Division (Airmobile); ARVN: airborne task force

Casualties   NVA: 1,044 killed; US: 92 killed

Key actions   The fifth day, April 5, opened with an enemy attack on Hill 471, which the Marines had occupied the previous afternoon. At 05:15 hours the 7th Battalion, 66th Regiment, 304th North Vietnamese Division, charged up the hill. The fight was one of the highlights of Operation Pegasus and was quite one-sided. Assisted by tremendous artillery and close air support, the Marines cut down large numbers of the attackers while suffering few casualties themselves.

Key effects   The rapid and successful conclusion of Operation Pegasus can be attributed first to detailed planning and preparation. Second, the enemy was either unable to, or did not know how to, react against airmobile maneuvering of large numbers of combat troops and supporting artillery around and behind their positions. Third, an unprecedented degree of bomber and fighter air support was provided to the ground forces, and this combat power punched the enemy along the front line and throughout positions to his rear.

A U.S. soldier signals to a hovering helicopter during Operation Pegasus in early April 1968.

This operation was a helicopter assault into the A Shau Valley to destroy North Vietnamese Army (NVA) bases located there. It began on the morning of April 19. Extensive B-52 air attacks and artillery bombardments paved the way for the initial air assault into the valley by the 3rd Brigade, 1st Cavalry Division. Nevertheless, the NVA antiaircraft fire that met the helicopter-borne troops was intense. To the east, the 1st Brigade, U.S. 101st Airborne Division, began its drive westward along Route 547. The U.S. 2d Battalion, 327th Infantry Regiment, attacked southwest along the road. They were followed by an air assault by the 1st Battalion, 327th Infantry Regiment, into a landing zone near the junction of Routes 547 and 547A.

Into the valley

The next day, the 3rd Brigade, 1st Cavalry Division, continued to send troops into the northern A Shau Valley as the 1st Battalion, 7th Cavalry, pushed southeast from their landing zone. In addition, the 5th Battalion, 7th Cavalry Regiment, moved to block Route 548, which entered the valley from Laos to the west. The communists were being squeezed from all directions. The 2d Battalion, 7th Cavalry, began an air assault to establish a landing zone further south in the valley. The ARVN 6th Airborne Battalion was airlanded into the valley by helicopter, and immediately made contact with the enemy upon moving out from the landing zone. By mid-May the enemy were defeated.

OPERATION DELAWARE

Location   Western Thua Thien Province, South Vietnam

Date   April 19–May 17, 1968

Commanders and forces   NVA; ARVN: 1st Army Division; U.S.: 1st Cavalry Division, 101st Airborne Division

Casualties   NVA: 869 killed; U.S.: 142 killed

Key actions   The link-up between the cavalry forces in the valley and those moving west along Routes 547 and 547A took place on May 12. Company C, 1st Battalion, 12th Cavalry, represented the valley elements while the 3rd Vietnamese Army Airborne Battalion was the lead unit in the westward moving forces.

Key effects   Any serious attempt by the enemy to conduct major offensive operations out of the A Shau base area would now require many months of additional preparations.

OPERATION ALLEN BROOK

By the beginning of May 1968 both the Marines at Da Nang and the communist forces in Quang Nam were in the middle of preparations to launch offensive operations against one another. On May 4, at 05:00 hours, Lieutenant Colonel Charles E. Mueller's 2d Battalion, 7th Marine Regiment, launched a two-company operation. In the first phase of the operation, which soon became Operation Allen Brook, the battalion encountered light but persistent resistance from enemy local forces and guerrilla units.

Battle at Phu Dong

About 09:00 hours on the morning of May 16, the 3rd Battalion encountered NVA troops in the hamlet of Phu Dong (2). By early evening, the Marine infantry who had fought continuously throughout the day in the oppressive heat, finally forced the NVA soldiers out of their trenches and bunkers. Afraid of encirclement, the enemy withdrew, leaving 130 dead at the hamlet.

Beginning with the action of May 16, the 7th and later the 27th Marine Regiments were involved in a series of battles against well dug-in and relatively fresh and well-trained North Vietnamese soldiers. For the entire operation through the end of May, the Marines reported to have killed over 600 of the enemy. They themselves sustained since the beginning of the operation 138 killed, 686 wounded, including 576 serious enough to be evacuated.

OPERATION ALLEN BROOK

Location   Quang Nam Province, South Vietnam

Date   May 4–August 24, 1968

Commanders and forces   NVA: 308th Division; ARVN: 51st Regiment; U.S. 1st Marine Division

Casualties   NVA: 1,017 killed; US: 172 killed

Key actions   Early on June 19, a force composed of elements of two U.S. Marine companies ran into a North Vietnamese force near the hamlet of Bac Dong Ban. The North Vietnamese were thoroughly dug in, occupying a line of trenches and bunkers with their backs to the Song Ky Lam. For nine hours, the battle raged with neither side able to gain the upper hand. By 19:00 hours, the Marines overwhelmed the enemy, suffering six dead, 19 wounded, and 12 heat casualties. By noon the next day, the Marines found 17 North Vietnamese dead.

Key effects   The Marines inflicted heavy casualties on the NVA, and hindered the communist build-up around Da Nang.

OPERATION MAMELUKE THRUST

Mameluke Thrust was a multi-regiment U.S. offensive campaign to destroy the growing communist threat to Da Nang from the west and southwest. The most intense action took place in the An Hoa Basin, where a saturation of patrols, ambushes, and coordinated company-sized search-and-clear operations put a high price on enemy attempts to use the area as an avenue of approach to Da Nang. Operating from hilltop-vantage points on the periphery of the basin, U.S. Marine reconnaissance teams interrupted enemy movements by calling in air strikes and artillery attacks. These inflicted many casualties.

OPERATION MAMELUKE THRUST

Location   Quang Nam Province, South Vietnam

Date   May 18–October 23, 1968

Commanders and forces   NVA; U.S.: 1st Marine Division

Casualties   NVA: 2,728 killed; U.S.: 270 killed

Key actions   During Mameluke Thrust operations, U.S. Marines made heavy contact with the enemy. The Marines killed 2,728 NVA and captured one. Numerous bunkers and caves were uncovered, particularly on operations in the Happy Valley area. Many of these sites were regimental size and showed evidence of recent occupation. Large amounts of ammunition, food, weapons, and documents were found.

Key effects   The communists cautiously avoided decisive contact, giving rise to the theory that they were saving their resources for another offensive. Rumors of an impending major attack by the enemy began to take on lives their own. The expected communist thrust was referred to variously as the "third offensive" (the Tet and the May offensives being the first and second, respectively), the "autumn offensive," or the "summer offensive."

An American patrol hunts for the elusive enemy in the hills to the west of the base of Da Nang.

COMMUNIST OFFENSIVE

American troops, supported by a tank, launch hand grenades at NVA forces during the 1969 communist offensive.

As in 1968, communist forces launched a major offensive throughout South Vietnam, one day after the end of the seven-day Viet Cong-proclaimed truce for Tet. The main enemy targets were U.S. and ARVN forces and installations in the Quang Nam lowlands, An Hoa industrial complex, Tam Ky City, the Tien Phuoc CIDG Camp, and Quang Ngai Province.

Enemy rocket and mortar fire also slammed into Saigon. The North Vietnamese Army (NVA) and Viet Cong (VC) achieved no military gains as the attacks were preempted by aggressive Allied sweeping operations. On February 23, the VC and NVA launched an offensive in the Mekong Delta region. For nearly a week the enemy continued to launch attacks against a number of U.S. targets in both isolated and urban areas. They were all defeated.

COMMUNIST OFFENSIVE	
Location	South Vietnam
Date	February 1969
Commanders and forces	NVA/VC: General Giap, U.S. and Allied: General William C. Westmoreland
Casualties	NVA: unknown; U.S.: 1,140 dead
Key actions	The heaviest fighting was around Saigon.
Key effects	The communists were one again made aware of the overwhelming power of U.S. aircraft and artillery.

HAMBURGER HILL

Also called the Battle of Ap Bia Mountain, this clash was part of Operation Apache Snow, a U.S. operation desinged to harry North Vietnamese Army (NVA) units in the A Shau Valley. On Hamburger Hill the NVA regulars decided to stand and fight. This created a bloody "meat-grinder" battle that led U.S. participants to call it "Hamburger Hill."

On the second day of the U.S. operation, soldiers of the 3rd Battalion, 187th Infantry Regiment, came under heavy NVA fire from troops positioned on Hill 937. Unconnected to the surrounding ridges, Hill 937 stood alone and, like the surrounding valley, was heavily forested.

After three days of fighting the battalion was reinforced by two more 101st Airborne Division battalions plus a battalion of the 3rd ARVN Regiment.

The bomb-blasted Hamburger Hill following its capture by American and ARVN troops in May 1969.

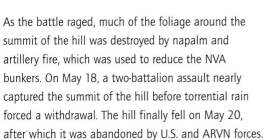

As the battle raged, much of the foliage around the summit of the hill was destroyed by napalm and artillery fire, which was used to reduce the NVA bunkers. On May 18, a two-battalion assault nearly captured the summit of the hill before torrential rain forced a withdrawal. The hill finally fell on May 20, after which it was abandoned by U.S. and ARVN forces.

HAMBURGER HILL

Location A Shau Valley, South Vietnam

Date May 11–20, 1969

Commanders and forces NVA: 6th, 9th, and 29th Regiments; U.S.: 101st Airborne Division; ARVN: 1st Division

Casualties NVA: 630 killed; U.S. & ARVN: 70 killed, 372 wounded

Key actions On May 20, after 10 previous assaults, a four-battalion attack drove the NVA defenders off the hill and into nearby Laos.

Key effects A controversy arose over taking a hill at great cost, only to abandon it for the communists to reoccupy. This led to the limiting of U.S. military operations in the face of troop withdrawals and Vietnamization.

OPERATION TOAN THANG

Hunting "Charlie" with rocket-armed helicopter gunships. Air support was crucial to U.S. and ARVN forces on the ground.

The Toan Thang operations (there were ultimately 11) were a series of massive operations throughout South Vietnam. They combined the forces of the ARVN's III Corps and the Americans' II Field Force. A total of 42 U.S. combat battalions participated at one time or another. A major aim was to discourage North Vietnamese Army (NVA) campsites and rocket positions within striking distance of Saigon. In early 1969 U.S. and ARVN forces discovered large quantities of enemy weapons, ammunition, and food in what was one of the biggest caches of munitions found during the war.

OPERATION TOAN THANG (COMPLETE VICTORY)

Location Saigon, Bien Hoa, Binh Duong, Binh Long, Binh Tuy, Gia Dinh, Hau Nghia, Long An, Long Khanh, Phuoc Long, Phuoc Tuy, and Tay Ninh Provinces, South Vietnam

Date April 1968–February 1969

Commanders and forces NVA/VC: VC 267th Local Force Battalion; U.S.: 1st Cavalry Division; 1st Infantry Division; 9th Infantry Division; 25th Infantry Division; 3rd Brigade, 101st Airborne Division; 199th Infantry Brigade (Light); 11th Armored Cavalry Regiment; Australia: 3rd Battalion, Royal Australian Regiment

Casualties NVA/VC: 2,549 killed; U.S.: 172 killed

Key actions The month of June saw daily contacts with small enemy units. American troops were locating and destroying small supply dumps, thus maintaining a strong and persistent offensive against the enemy. A major contact was sustained on June 17, 1968. Elements of the 2d Battalion, 27th Infantry Regiment, were located in a night camp which received a main attack by an estimated NVA battalion employing small arms, rockets, and mortars. Immediately the U.S. troops returned fire with weapons, artillery, and gunships. The NVA battalion had to withdraw, leaving 67 dead and a large amount of weapons, munitions, and personal gear behind.

Key effects The Americans captured 100,000 rifles, 643 mortars, and 35,000 rounds for heavy machine guns.

As the United States began a withdrawal from the war in Vietnam and turned the fighting over to the Army of the Republic of Vietnam (ARVN), dramatic events occurred. These were the crossborder raids into Cambodia, aimed at destroying the North Vietnamese Army's (NVA's) sanctuaries. However, the raids were largely disappointing in their results in terms of numbers of enemy casualties. Back in the United States, though, these raids had an explosive effect on dozens of college campuses, as students staged large-scale demonstrations. These strengthened the antiwar movement and led to bloodshed on U.S. soil.

American withdrawal

As the United States' policy of Vietnamization went forward, the U.S. casualty rate fell. As the ground war wound down, the air war was meanwhile still inflicting punishing casualties on the enemy. U.S. Air Force (USAF) B-52 bombers and tactical aircraft, plus U.S. Navy and Marine fighter-bombers, continued to interdict the flow of supplies coming down the Ho Chi Minh Trail, as well as hitting enemy troop concentrations in Laos and Cambodia. Also targeted by U.S. and South Vietnamese aircraft were enemy troop concentrations inside South Vietnam itself. By the end of 1970, U.S. and South Vietnamese aircraft had disrupted North Vietnam's ability to launch Tet-style offensives.

The success of the Allied tactics, both on the ground and in the air, against the sanctuaries in Laos and Cambodia, as well as the interdiction campaign aimed at the Ho Chi Minh Trail, forced the North Vietnamese to revert to guerrilla-style tactics. However, these tactics, first applied back in the early 1960s, now failed, as pacification efforts by the U.S. Marines and ARVN paid huge dividends among the South Vietnamese peasants. This was illustrated by the increase in the number of attacks the NVA and rebuilt Viet Cong (VC) aimed at villages and hamlets.

A U.S. AH-1 Cobra gunship in South Vietnam. Its narrow shape meant it could hide down low amongst the trees if needed.

Combined U.S. and ARVN pressure ensured that the NVA was kept on the defensive throughout 1970.

Even as the war became "Vietnamized," the NVA and VC reverted to a campaign of terrorism and intimidation against South Vietnamese civilians in a renewed bid to undermine the confidence and stability of President Thieu's government. As the United States turned its attention to ending the war and domestic political problems brought on by the Watergate scandal (1973–1974), Hanoi launched a major offensive during March and April 1972, known as the "Easter Offensive." Supported by U.S. ground advisors and aircraft flying nonstop air support strikes against waves of North Vietnamese tanks and armored vehicles, the ARVN put up a spirited defense and later launched a series of offensive operations that forced the North Vietnamese to seek a de facto armistice. Determined to be re-elected and finally end the Vietnam War, President Richard M. Nixon and his National Security Advisor, Henry Kissinger, used both force and diplomacy in their bid to end the conflict and achieve what the president called "peace with honor." Using both a "velvet glove" (diplomacy) and an "iron fist" (a massive bombing campaign) aimed at Hanoi itself during Christmas 1972, the United States finally brought an uneasy lull to the war in 1973.

The fall of the South

Between 1971 and 1974, the bulk of U.S. ground and air forces departed South Vietnam and turned the war over to the ARVN. At the same time, the North was gearing up its war effort. The Paris Peace Accords signed in January 1973 seemed to guarantee the survival of South Vietnam, but the communists had no intention of ending the war. They believed that victory was close (they were right in this assumption). In addition, each side accused the other of violating the truce. Fighting therefore continued. But with the withdrawal of U.S. forces, the South lacked air support to blunt the NVA. When the North launched a major offensive in early 1975, the ARVN crumbled and the NVA rolled into Saigon. The Vietnam War had ended in a communist victory.

In April 1970, ARVN and U.S. Army forces carried out huge search-and-destroy operations in a dozen base areas in Cambodia. A U.S.–Vietnamese naval task force also swept up the Mekong Delta in order to reopen a supply line to Phnom Penh, the Cambodian capital.

President Richard M. Nixon announced that several thousand American troops supporting the Cambodian invasion had entered Cambodia's "Fishook" area bordering South Vietnam in order to attack the location of the headquarters of the communist military operation in South Vietnam. American advisors, tactical air support, medical evacuation teams, and logistical support were also provided to support the incursion.

In support of the Cambodian operation was Brigade B from the Vietnamese Marine Corps which, on May 9, crossed the Cambodian border and at 09:30 hours landed at Neck Luong to began its phase of the operation. ARVN troops in Cambodia were increased to 50,000 by May 6. Withdrawal of the American units from Cambodia was complete when the 1st Cavalry

Division (Airmobile) returned to South Vietnam on June 30. However, this massive display of force achieved very little overall.

South Vietnamese and American soldiers deep inside Cambodia in 1970. Despite the use of tens of thousands of Allied soldiers, the invasion failed to destroy the communist network in Cambodia.

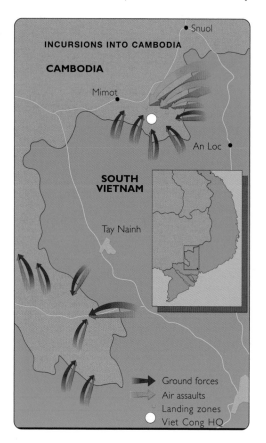

INCURSIONS INTO CAMBODIA

CAMBODIA

Snuol

Mimot

An Loc

SOUTH VIETNAM

Tay Nainh

→ Ground forces
⇒ Air assaults
○ Landing zones
● Viet Cong HQ

INCURSIONS INTO CAMBODIA

Location Cambodia

Date April 29–June 30, 1970

Commanders and forces NVA/VC; ARVN: 50,000 troops (9th, 21st, 22d, 23rd, Divisions, 3rd Airborne Brigade, Marine Corps); U.S.: 30,000 troops (3rd Brigade, 1st Cavalry Division; 11th Armored Cavalry Regiment; 4th Infantry Division)

Casualties NVA/VC: 10,000 killed; U.S: 338 killed; ARVN: 638 killed

Key actions On May 7, elements of the U.S. Army's 2d Brigade, 1st Cavalry Division (Airmobile), engaged an enemy force while operating in Cambodia 24 miles (38.6 km) northwest of Phuoc Binh. The air cavalrymen exchanged small-arms and automatic weapons fire with the NVA. Once again, US forces were supported by artillery, helicopter gunships, an Air Force AC-119 gunship, and tactical air strikes by the U.S. Air Force. The enemy lost 24 soldiers killed in action, while the U.S. suffered 8 killed in action. An aviation element from the U.S. 4th Infantry Division observed a platoon-sized enemy force in a large bunker and hut complex, 48 miles (77 km) northwest of Pleiku City, about 2 miles (3.2 km) inside Cambodia. The helicopter crew called in close air support, and U.S. Air Force jets killed 15 enemy soldiers and destroyed 63 bunkers.

Key effects The combined U.S. and Armed Forces of the Republic of Vietnam operations in Cambodia indicated 10,000 enemy killed. In addition, 9,081 individual weapons, 1,283 crew-served weapons, and 5,400 tonnes (5,314 tons) of rice were captured or destroyed. The totals were exclusive of those predominantly RVNAF operations continuing or concluded in the "Parrot's Beak" area, Se San Base Areas, and the Mekong River Corridor. In view of the massive efforts involved, the Cambodian incursions were somewhat of a disappointment.

OPERATION LAM SON 719

Designed to cut enemy infiltration routes and to destroy North Vietnamese staging areas in Laos, American aviation units airlifted South Vietnamese troops into Laos.

In Lam Son 719, the Vietnamese hoped to disrupt Viet Cong and North Vietnamese supply lines by a combination of helicopter and armor ground attacks. The main attack was to be conducted along National Highway 9 to Aloui by airborne troops and the 1st Armored Brigade, which would then continue west. The South Vietnamese 1st Infantry Division, in a series of airmobile assaults, established fire bases on the high ground south of Route 9 to secure the south flank. The South Vietnamese 1st Ranger Group carried out airmobile assaults to establish blocking positions and secure the north flank. The operation inflicted a large number of casualties on the North Vietnamese Army. However, American commanders were not impressed by the performance of the ARVN, giving them little hope that it would be able to repel any North Vietnamese invasion of the South.

OPERATION LAM SON 719

Location southeast Laos

Date February 8–March 25, 1971

Commanders and forces NVA: 48th, 243rd, 812th Regiment, plus 5,000 Laotian troops; ARVN: 1st Infantry Division, 1st Armored Brigade; U.S.: 1st Battalion, 61st Infantry Regiment, 1st Battalion, 77th Armor, 3rd Squadron, 5th Cavalry Regiment, 4th Squadron, 12th Cavalry Regiment

Casualties NVA: 13,000 killed; ARVN: 1,529killed, 5,483 wounded, 625 missing; U.S.: 215 killed, 1,149 wounded

Key actions On February 25 the NVA made an armored attack against Fire Base 31. They had moved their armor over concealed routes to final assault positions before being discovered. Then the tanks with supporting infantry launched a violent daylight attack against the fire base. The defenders, supported by U.S. aircraft, threw back the first and second waves of the enemy attack; but, on the third wave, three Soviet-made T-34 tanks made it into the base and forced the withdrawal of the defenders. This was to be the first and last success of enemy tanks during Lam Son 719 and the only friendly fire base to be completely overrun in Laos.

Key effects The fighting was to be done by the Vietnamese, in a major test of President Nixon's policy of "Vietnamizing" the American-led war. Despite heavy U.S. aerial, logistical, and artillery support, Saigon's troops were badly defeated. While North Vietnamese supply routes were briefly disrupted, the six-week operation exposed Vietnamization as an illusory escape hatch for salvaging a failing policy. Lam Son 719 demonstrated what can happen when a large operation is insufficiently coordinated: conflicting orders were issued, the limited amount of armor was misused, unit leadership broke down, and the strength of the enemy was either overlooked or disregarded.

AIR STRIKES AGAINST THE NORTH

In February 1971, the U.S. Air Force (USAF) began a series of offensives against North Vietnam. On March 21–22, the USAF teamed up with the Navy in Operation Fracture Cross Alpha, during which they flew 234 strike and 20 armed reconnaissance sorties against enemy surface-to-air missile (SAM) sites. In August 1971, in an effort to curb enemy road construction across the border into South Vietnam, USAF jets flew 473 sorties. On September 21, flying in poor weather, 196 U.S. aircraft hit three fuel storage

areas south of Dong Hoi, destroying tens of thousands of gallons of fuel. Frustrated over Hanoi's refusal to talk, as well as by stalling at the Paris Peace Talks, in November 1971 President Nixon authorized the U.S. Air Force and the Navy to resume their bombing missions over North Vietnam.

AIR STRIKES AGAINST THE NORTH

Location North Vietnam

Date February–November, 1971

Commanders and forces North Vietnam: 250 fighter aircraft; USAF and U.S. Navy

Casualties unknown

Key actions On November 7–8, USAF and U.S. Navy pilots bombed airfields at Dong Hoi, Vinh, and Quan Lang. After neutralizing these air bases, U.S. pilots on December 26–30 launched the heaviest air strikes since 1968. Some 1,025 sorties attacked a variety of military targets in North Vietnam.

Key effects It became obvious that the North Vietnamese were not impressed by the U.S. bombing campaign. By the end of 1971 it looked like the North Vietnamese were poised for a major operation against the South.

In late August 1970, intelligence reports indicated that the Viet Cong (VC) Front 4 Headquarters had taken up residence in the eastern Que Son Mountains. In response, the 7th Marine Regiment planned to begin Operation Imperial Lake in this area to destroy it. The bombardment began at midnight on August 31. For six hours, Marine artillery fired more than 14,000 shells in what was one of the largest artillery barrages of the entire Vietnam War. When the artillery fire ceased, two solid hours of air strikes followed.

Hard fighting

By September 9, the Marines had suffered three killed and a dozen wounded. The Marines pulled back and called for air support. Nine sorties dropped bombs and rockets on the enemy. The next day the Marines encountered only sporadic sniper fire. The companies spent the next week searching for any surviving VC, killing more than a dozen stragglers.

During the operation the Marines uncovered a large underground complex consisting of more than the usual caves. Extending more than 70 ft (21 m) into the ground, the complex included a large kitchen and a hospital complete with an operating room. What made the find even more unusual was the fact that the complex was on the lower slopes of Hill 845, right below two Marine landing zones. Imperial Lake was the last major U.S. Marine operation in Vietnam.

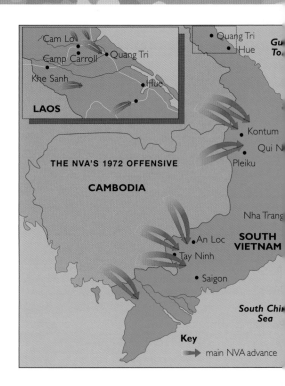

THE NVA'S 1972 OFFENSIVE

Key
→ main NVA advance

A major North Vietnamese offensive, the "Easter Offensive" began on March 30. The total U.S. military strength in the South was 95,000 military personnel, of which only 6,000 were combat troops. The task of countering the offensive fell almost entirely to the ARVN. The North Vietnamese Army (NVA) poured across the Demilitarized Zone (DMZ) and out of bases inside Laos. By the late summer the "Easter Offensive" was over. What turned the tide of victory for the ARVN was the use of massive U.S. air support.

OPERATION IMPERIAL LAKE

Location Quang Nam Province, South Vietnam

Date August 31, 1970–May 12, 1971

Commanders and forces VC: unknown; U.S.: 1st Marine Division

Casualties VC: 305 killed; U.S.: 24 killed

Key actions On September 5, Marine Company E encountered a platoon of communists in a jungle-covered ravine southwest of LZ Vulture. Unable to move deeper into the ravine due to the heavy volume of fire coming from enemy soldiers concealed in caves and behind boulders, Company E was joined by the other three companies that night. Over the next four days, the Marines fought the encircled enemy. The steep terrain, numerous boulders, thick foliage, and many caves favored the enemy's elusive tactics. Although the riflemen tried several times to advance along the bottom of the ravine or down its sides, they were turned back each time by strong small arms and automatic weapons fire.

Key effects This was the last major U.S. Marine operation in the Vietnam War.

NVA EASTER OFFENSIVE

Location South Vietnam

Date March 30–October 22, 1972

Commanders and forces NVA; ARVN

Casualties NVA: 40,000 killed plus 450 tanks destroyed; ARVN: 10,000 killed

Key actions On June 19, a South Vietnamese counteroffensive began in Military Region 2.

Key effects Although South Vietnamese forces withstood their greatest trial thus far in the conflict, the North Vietnamese accomplished two important goals. They had gained valuable territory within South Vietnam from which to launch any future offensives. This was half of the four northernmost provinces—Quang Tri, Thua Thien, Quang Nam, and Quang Tin—as well as the western fringes of the II and III Corps sectors (around 10 percent of the country). They had also obtained a better bargaining position at the peace negotiations being conducted in Paris.

OPERATION LINEBACKER II

Operation Linebacker II flights were initiated on December 18, 1972. The primary objective of the bombing operation would be to force the North Vietnamese Government to enter into purposeful negotiations concerning a ceasefire agreement. The operation employed air power to its maximum capabilities in an attempt to destroy all major target complexes such as radio stations, railroads, power plants, and airfields located in the Hanoi and Haiphong areas. Unlike previous bombing campaigns, Linebacker II provided the U.S. Air Force (USAF) and U.S. Navy forces with specific objectives and removed many of the restrictions that had previously caused much frustration among pilots.

Pounding North Vietnam

During these operations, USAF and navy aircraft and B-52 bombers commenced an around-the-clock bombardment of the North Vietnamese heartland. The B-52s struck Hanoi and Haiphong during hours of darkness, with F-111s and Navy tactical aircraft providing diversionary/suppression strikes on airfields and surface-to-air missile (SAM) sites. Daylight operations were primarily carried out by A-7s and F-4s.

This railroad bridge in North Vietnam was hit by bombs several times during Operation Linebacker II.

Between December 18 and 22 the U.S. Navy conducted 119 Linebacker II strikes in North Vietnam. The attack effort was concentrated in the Haiphong area. Strikes were conducted against SAM sites, anti-aircraft artillery installations, railroads and highways, Thanh Hoa Army barracks, the Haiphong Naval Base, petroleum centers, and other military related targets.

By December 29, 1972, the 700 nighttime sorties flown by B-52s and 650 daytime strikes by fighter and attack aircraft had persuaded the North Vietnamese Government to return to the conference table. However, even after Linebacker II had ended American aircraft continued to attack the North until a ceasefire came into effect in January 1973.

OPERATION LINEBACKER II

Location North Vietnam

Date December 18–29, 1972

Commanders and forces North Vietnam: 250 fighters; U.S. Air Force, U.S. Navy

Casualties Overall U.S. Air Force losses included 15 B-52s, two F-4s, two F-111s, and one HH-53 search and rescue helicopter. Navy losses included two A-7s, two A-6s, one RA-5, and one F-4. Seventeen of these losses were attributed to SAM missiles, three to daytime MiG attacks, three to antiaircraft artillery, and three to unknown causes.

Key actions Heavy raids around Hanoi, which resumed the day after the Christmas bombing halt, were eased as the North showed indications of returning to the conference table.

Key effects The impact of the bombing was obvious in the severe damage caused to North Vietnamese military targets.

By March 1973 all U.S. ground forces had left Vietnam, while North Vietnamese Army (NVA) forces remained in South Vietnam. Most ARVN commanders realized that, with the U.S. withdrawal, it was only a matter of time before the NVA would act. Despite the fact that the ARVN had held its own during the North's Easter Offensive, only with U.S. air power could the South Vietnamese push back the NVA. As the events of 1975 indicated, the refusal of the U.S. to intervene doomed South Vietnam and its infant republic to the tanks and guns of the NVA. The NVA waited for the signal to strike south in what it thought would be a two-year campaign. Much to its surprise, the conquest took just four months.

The North strikes

The seizure of Phuoc Long Province on January 6, 1975, signaled the beginning of the end. Located north of Saigon, Phuoc Long was isolated and practically encircled by enemy forces for months before its capture. Supplies had to be flown in or delivered by armed convoys. Phuoc Long was considered by ARVN commanders to be weakly defended.

The NVA's seizure of Phuoc Long was designed to test the will of the South's armed forces and to gauge the reaction of the U.S. The fall of Phuoc Long was the first time in the Vietnam War that an entire province had been lost to the communists. It was a clear violation of the ceasefire agreement by the communists, yet ARVN forces chose not to react militarily, while the U.S. made no significant move to deter the communists. In the words of South Vietnamese President Nguyen Van Thieu, while it was not "impossible to reoccupy Phuoc Long," from a military standpoint, "it was not worthwhile" as it would have drained troops from other critical areas.

The fall of the South

On March 10, the NVA attacked Ban Me Thuot at the start of its 1975 Spring Offensive. On March 19, the South Vietnamese Army abandoned Quang Tri City and its province. On March 24, Quang Ngai City and Tam Ky fell to the advancing NVA. The next day, Hue City was captured by the NVA. On March 30, the NVA entered Da Nang City and captured the Da Nang Air Base. There was almost no resistance to the communists. The ARVN was collapsing. On the last day of April the North Vietnamese Army entered Saigon (which was quickly renamed Ho Chi Minh City) and arrested the president. The Vietnam War was finally over.

THE FALL OF THE SOUTH

Location   South Vietnam

Date   March 10–April 30, 1975

Commanders and forces   NVA; ARVN

Casualties   More than 200,000 South Vietnamese government officials, military officers, and soldiers were sent to "reeducation camps," where torture, disease, and malnutrition were widespread.

Key actions   American military aid to the government of South Vietnam was cut from over $2.5 billion in fiscal year 1973 to $700 million in fiscal year 1975. South Vietnamese vulnerability was due to the the lack of a mobile reserve and strategic mobility due to shortages of fuel, transport, and spares. Their soldiers had been conditioned by the U.S. to rely on massive air and artillery support in combat and had forgotten how to think for themselves when military resources became increasingly scarce after the Paris Agreements and American support decreased.

Key effects   The whole of Vietnam became a communist state.

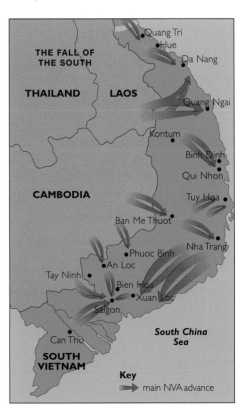

FURTHER RESOURCES

PUBLICATIONS

Anzenberger, Joseph F., Jr., *Combat Art of the Vietnam War*, Mcfarland & Co. Inc. Publishers, Jefferson, NC, 1986.

Bender, David L., *Indochina War: Why Our Policy Failed*, Greenhaven Press, Chicago, IL, 1975.

Brenner, Samuel, *Living Through the Vietnam War*, Greenhaven Press, Chicago, IL, 2005.

Brownell, Richard, *History's Great Defeats—America's Failure in Vietnam*, Lucent Books, Chicago, IL, 2005.

Burgan, Michael. *The Vietnam War (Witness to History)*, Heinemann, Oxford, UK, 2004.

Caputo, Philip, *10,000 Days of Thunder: A History of the Vietnam War*, Atheneum, New York, 2005.

Dolan, Edward F., *America After Vietnam: Legacies of a Hated War*, Franklin Watts, London, UK, 1989.

Fitzgerald, Brian, *Fighting The Vietnam War*, Raintree, Oxford, UK, 2005.

Galt, Margot Fortunato, *Stop This War: American Protest of the Conflict in Vietnam*, Lerner Publishing Group, Minneapolis, MN, 2000.

Gifford, Clive, *How Did It Happen?—The Vietnam War*, Lucent Books, Chicago, IL, 2005.

Hazen, Walter A., *Vietnam War*, Instructional Fair, Grand Rapids, MI, 1999.

Kent, Deborah, *The Vietnam War: "What Are We Fighting For?" (American War Series)*, Enslow Publishers, New York, 2000.

Levy, Debbie, *The Vietnam War (Chronicle of America's Wars)*, Lerner Publications, Minneapolis, MN, 2004.

MacLear, Michael, *The 10,000 Day War: Vietnam*, St Martins Press, New York, 1981.

Marcovitz, Hal, *The Vietnam War (World History)*, Lucent Books, Chicago, IL, 2007.

Mason, Andrew, *The Vietnam War: A Primary Source History (In Their Own Words)*, Gareth Stevens Publishing, Strongsville, OH, 2005.

Murray, Stuart, *Vietnam War Battles & Leaders*, DK Children, New York, 2004

Rice, Earle, *Point of No Return: Tonkin Gulf and the Vietnam War (First Battles)*, Morgan Reynolds Publishing, Greensboro, NC, 2003.

Rice, Earle, *Weapons of War: The Vietnam War (American War Library)*, Lucent Books, Chicago, IL, 2000.

Roleff, Tamara L., *History Firsthand—The Vietnam War*, Greenhaven Press, 2001.

Schomp, Virginia, *The Vietnam War (Letters from the Homefront)*, Benchmark Books, New York, 2009.

Schynert, Mark, *Women in History—Women of the Vietnam War*, Lucent Books, Chicago, IL, 2004.

Shane-Armstrong, R., *Great Speeches in History—The Vietnam War*, Greenhaven Press, Chicago, IL, 2004.

Summers, Harry G., *The Vietnam War Almanac,* Facts on File, New York, 1985.

Warren, James A., *Portrait of a Tragedy: America and the Vietnam War*, Lothrop Lee & Shepard, New York, 1990.

Wiest, Andrew, *The Vietnam War*, Rosen Publishing Group, New York, 2008.

Wright, David K., *Causes and Consequences of the Vietnam War*, Raintree Steck-Vaughn Publishers, Wilmington, MA, 1995.

Yancey, Diane, *Life of an American Soldier in Vietnam*, Lucent Books, Chicago, IL, 2000.

WEBSITES

www.vietnampix.com
A pictorial guide to the whole conflict.

www.vietnamwar.com
The ultimate resource for the Vietnam War.

www.pbs.org/battlefieldvietnam
The battles of the Vietnam War.

http://vietnam.vassar.edu
An overview of the conflict in Vietnam, 1945 to 1975.

www.vietnam-war.info
Facts about the Vietnam War.

www.vhfcn.org/stat.html
Statistics about the Vietnam War.

www.spartacus.schoolnet.co.uk/VietnamWar.htm
Overview of the Vietnam War.

INDEX